Recipes: The Cooking of Germany

Contents

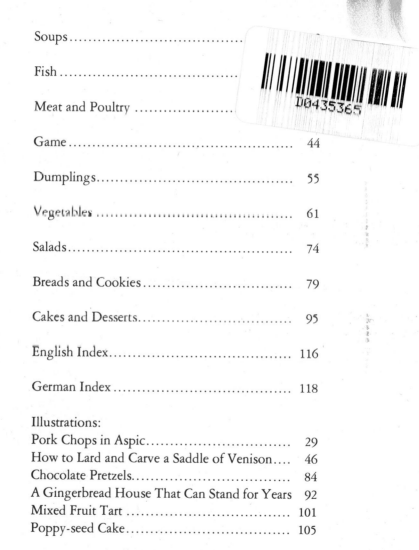

Soups ....

Fish ....

Meat and Poultry ....

Game 44

Dumplings 55

Vegetables 61

Salads 74

Breads and Cookies 79

Cakes and Desserts 95

English Index 116

German Index 118

Illustrations:
Pork Chops in Aspic 29
How to Lard and Carve a Saddle of Venison 46
Chocolate Pretzels 84
A Gingerbread House That Can Stand for Years 92
Mixed Fruit Tart 101
Poppy-seed Cake 105

Foods of the World

TIME-LIFE BOOKS, NEW YORK

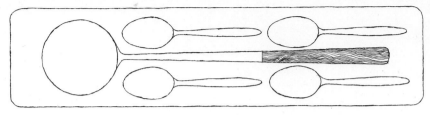

Graupensuppe mit Hühnerklein
CHICKEN GIBLET AND BARLEY SOUP

To serve 4 to 6

2 pounds chicken wings, necks and
  backs
2 pounds chicken hearts and
  gizzards, coarsely chopped
2 quarts cold water; or 1 quart
  chicken stock, fresh or canned,
  combined with 1 quart water
2 carrots, scraped and coarsely
  chopped
2 celery stalks, including the leaves,
  coarsely chopped

1 small parsnip, scraped and coarsely
  chopped
1 onion, peeled and pierced with 2
  whole cloves
Freshly ground black pepper
¼ cup dried mushrooms, coarsely
  chopped
½ cup boiling water
½ cup pearl barley, thoroughly
  rinsed in cold water
2 tablespoons finely chopped fresh
  parsley

In a 5-quart saucepan or soup pot, combine the chicken wings, necks, backs, hearts and gizzards with the water or stock and water. Bring to a boil over high heat, skimming off all the foam and scum as they rise to the surface. Add the carrots, celery, parsnip, onion with the cloves, and a few grindings of pepper. Reduce the heat to low, partially cover the pan and simmer gently for 30 minutes. Meanwhile, in a small bowl, cover the chopped mushrooms with ½ cup boiling water and let them soak for 30 minutes. Then add them with their soaking liquid to the soup and pour in the barley. Stirring occasionally, simmer half covered for 1 hour, or until the barley, giblets and mushrooms are tender.

    Remove the wings, necks and backs from the soup with a slotted spoon. Skin them and pick the meat from the bones. Chop the meat coarsely and add it to the simmering soup. Discard the onion. Taste for seasoning and stir in the parsley. Serve from a heated tureen or a large serving bowl.

Linsensuppe
LENTIL SOUP

To serve 6

2 cups dried quick-cooking lentils
2 quarts cold water
¼ pound lean bacon in 1 piece
1 leek, white part plus 2 inches of green, finely chopped
1 large carrot, scraped and finely chopped
1 parsnip, scraped and finely chopped
1 celery stalk, finely chopped
2 tablespoons bacon fat
½ cup finely chopped onions
2 tablespoons flour
2 tablespoons cider vinegar (optional)
2 frankfurters, sliced into ¼-inch rounds
1 teaspoon salt
Freshly ground black pepper

Wash the lentils thoroughly under cold running water. In a heavy 4-quart casserole bring 2 quarts of water to a boil over high heat. Add the lentils, the piece of bacon, and the chopped leek, carrot, parsnip and celery. Return to a boil, reduce the heat to low, and simmer, partially covered, for 30 minutes.

Melt 2 tablespoons of bacon fat over moderate heat in a heavy 8- to 10-inch skillet and when it begins to splutter, add the chopped onions. Cook, stirring occasionally, for 8 to 10 minutes, or until the onions are soft and lightly colored. Sprinkle the flour over them, lower the heat and cook, stirring constantly, until the flour turns a golden brown. Watch carefully for any sign of burning and regulate the heat accordingly. Ladle about ½ cup of the simmering lentil soup into the browned flour and beat vigorously with a whisk until the mixture is smooth and thick. Stir in the vinegar, if you are using it. Then, with a spatula, scrape the entire contents of the skillet into the lentils and stir together thoroughly.

Cover the casserole and simmer over low heat for another 30 minutes, or until the lentils are tender but not mushy. Before serving, cut the bacon into small dice and return it to the soup with the sliced frankfurters. Simmer for 2 or 3 minutes to heat the meat through, then stir in the salt and a few grindings of black pepper.

If the soup is to be served as a main dish, increase the number of frankfurters as necessary.

Heisse Biersuppe
HOT BEER SOUP

To serve 4

3 twelve-ounce bottles or cans of
   light beer
½ cup sugar

4 egg yolks
⅓ cup sour cream
½ teaspoon ground cinnamon
¼ teaspoon salt
Freshly ground black pepper

Pour beer and sugar into a heavy 4- to 5-quart saucepan. Bring to a boil over high heat, stirring constantly until the sugar is dissolved, then remove the pan from the heat. In a small bowl, beat the egg yolks with a wire whisk or fork to break them up, and beat in the sour cream a little at a time. Stir about ¼ cup of the hot beer into the mixture, and then whisk it into the beer. Add the cinnamon, salt and a few grindings of pepper. Return the pan to low heat and cook, stirring constantly, until the soup thickens slightly. Do not let it boil or it may curdle.

Taste for seasoning and serve at once from a heated tureen or in individual soup bowls.

Gaisburger Marsch
VEGETABLE-BEEF SOUP WITH TINY DUMPLINGS

To serve 4

1 pound boneless beef chuck, cut
   into 1-inch cubes
1 pound beef marrow bones, sawed,
   not chopped, into 1-inch pieces
2 quarts cold water
1 large onion, peeled and pierced
   with 2 whole cloves
1 small bay leaf
1 teaspoon salt

Freshly ground black pepper
1 cup coarsely diced peeled celery
   root
½ cup coarsely diced scraped carrots
½ cup coarsely diced scraped
   parsnips
1 cup coarsely diced leeks, including
   2 inches of the green top
2½ cups coarsely diced potatoes
One recipe *Spätzle (page 55)*
1 tablespoon finely chopped parsley

In a heavy 5- to 6-quart flameproof casserole or soup pot, bring the beef, bones and water to a boil over high heat, skimming off the foam and scum as they rise to the surface. Reduce the heat to the lowest possible point, add the onion pierced with cloves, bay leaf, salt and a few grindings of pepper, and simmer, partially covered, for 1½ hours, skimming whenever necessary. Then remove the onion and bay leaf, discard them, and transfer the bones to a plate.

With a small spoon or the tip of a knife, scoop out the marrow from the bones, add it to the soup and discard the bones. Add the celery root, carrots, parsnips, leeks and potatoes and simmer, undisturbed for 30 minutes, or until the vegetables and meat are tender. Stir the *Spätzle* into the simmering soup and cook for 1 or 2 minutes longer to heat them through. Then add the parsley, taste for seasoning, and serve either from a large heated tureen or in individual soup bowls.

Feine Kartoffelsuppe mit Gurken
POTATO SOUP WITH CUCUMBER

To serve 6

1 medium-sized or 2 small
   cucumbers
6 medium-sized boiling potatoes
   (about 2 pounds), peeled and cut
   into ½-inch dice
3 cups cold water
1½ teaspoons salt

¼ teaspoon freshly ground black
   pepper
1 cup heavy cream
1 cup milk
1 tablespoon grated onion
1 tablespoon finely chopped fresh
   dill, or substitute 1 teaspoon dried
   dill weed

With a small, sharp knife, peel the cucumber and slice it lengthwise into halves. Scoop out the seeds by running the tip of a teaspoon down the center of each half. Cut the cucumber into ¼-inch dice and set aside.

In a heavy 3- to 4-quart saucepan, bring the potatoes and water to a boil over high heat. Reduce the heat to moderate, add the salt and pepper and cook uncovered until the potatoes are soft and can easily be mashed against the sides of the pan; then pour them and all the cooking liquid into a sieve set over a mixing bowl. With a large spoon force the potatoes through the sieve. (If you prefer, purée the potatoes in a food mill. But don't use a blender; it will make the mixture too smooth.) However you have puréed the potatoes, return them and their liquid to the saucepan and stir in the cream, milk, grated onion and cucumbers. Simmer over low heat for about 5 minutes, or until the cucumber is tender but still somewhat firm. Add the dill and taste for seasoning. Serve hot either from a heated tureen or in individual soup bowls.

Blumenkohlsuppe

CREAM OF CAULIFLOWER SOUP

To serve 4

1 large cauliflower (about 1½
   pounds)
2 cups chicken stock, fresh or canned
2 cups cold water
4 tablespoons butter

⅓ cup flour
1 cup milk
1 teaspoon salt
¼ teaspoon white pepper
⅛ teaspoon ground nutmeg
1 egg yolk
¼ teaspoon fresh lemon juice

Cut away the thick stem at the base of the cauliflower and tear off the green leaves. Separate the flowerets and wash them under cold running water. Reserve 10 small flowerets, and chop the rest coarsely. Combine the stock and water in a 2- to 3-quart saucepan, and bring to a boil over high heat. Drop in the whole flowerets, and boil briskly, uncovered, for 10 minutes, or until they are tender but still somewhat resistant to the point of a small, sharp knife. Remove the flowerets and set them aside in a bowl. Reserve the stock.

Melt the butter over moderate heat in a 4-quart stainless-steel or enameled saucepan. Stir in the flour and cook over low heat, stirring constantly, for 1 or 2 minutes. Do not let the flour brown. Pour in the stock and the milk, beating constantly with a whisk. Cook, stirring, until the mixture comes to a boil and is smooth and somewhat thick. Reduce the heat to low, and simmer for 2 or 3 minutes. Then add the chopped cauliflower, salt, pepper and nutmeg. Simmer, half covered, for 15 minutes, or until the cauliflower is soft enough to be easily mashed against the side of the pan. Pour the cauliflower and all of its cooking liquid into a sieve set over a bowl. With a wooden spoon, force the cauliflower through the sieve. (If you prefer, purée the cauliflower in a food mill. Don't use a blender; it will make the mixture too smooth.) Return the purée to the pan. Beat the egg yolk with a fork or whisk to break it up, then beat in ½ cup of hot purée, 2 tablespoons at a time. Now whisk the mixture back into the saucepan. Add the reserved flowerets and cook over moderate heat for 2 or 3 minutes, stirring occasionally. Do not let it boil. Add the lemon juice, taste for seasoning, and serve.

Fish

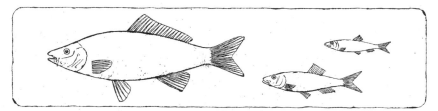

Zander Schnitte mit Senfbutter
FILLET OF WALLEYED PIKE WITH MUSTARD BUTTER

To serve 4

2 pounds medium-sized boiling
  potatoes, scrubbed but not
  peeled
2 pounds walleyed pike fillets,
  or substitute any other
  firm, white fresh-water fish
  fillets

1 tablespoon fresh lemon juice
½ teaspoon salt
¼ pound (1 stick) plus 6
  tablespoons butter
1 cup finely chopped onions
3 tablespoons Düsseldorf-
  style prepared mustard, or
  substitute 3 tablespoons
  other hot prepared mustard

Preheat the oven to 350°. Drop the potatoes into enough lightly salted boiling water to cover them completely. Boil them briskly, uncovered, for 20 to 30 minutes, or until they show no resistance when pierced with the tip of a small, sharp knife.

Meanwhile, wash the fillets under cold running water and pat them dry with paper towels. Sprinkle both sides of the fish with lemon juice and salt and let them rest for 10 minutes. Then, melt 6 tablespoons of the butter in a shallow flameproof baking dish large enough to hold the fillets in one layer. Dip the fillets in the melted butter, turning to coat them thoroughly on both sides and arrange them side by side in the dish. Strew the chopped onions over them and bake in the middle of the oven for 12 to 15 minutes, or until the fish is firm and opaque. Do not overcook.

Drain and peel the potatoes and slice them crosswise into rounds ¼ inch thick. Arrange the slices in concentric circles, each slice slightly overlapping the other, on the bottom of a deep, heated serving platter. With a large spatula, carefully transfer the fish from its baking dish to the top of the potatoes. Pour any liquid remaining in the dish over the fish. Quickly melt the remaining ¼ pound of butter in a small saucepan, without letting it brown. When the butter foams, beat the mustard into it with a whisk and, while it is still foaming, pour it over the fish and potatoes, and serve at once.

Zander im Ofen gebacken mit Weisswein
WALLEYED PIKE BAKED IN WHITE WINE

To serve 4

2 tablespoons butter, softened, plus
    ¼ pound (1 stick), melted
A 3- to 3½-pound whole walleyed
    pike, cleaned and scaled but with
    head and tail left on, or substitute
    any other whole, firm, white fresh-
    water fish
1 teaspoon salt
1 tablespoon fresh lemon juice
1 medium-sized potato, peeled
2 slices bacon, 8 to 9 inches long

⅛ teaspoon white pepper
1 tablespoon finely chopped onions
3 whole allspice, 3 whole cloves
    and 3 whole black peppercorns,
    coarsely crushed with a mortar
    and pestle or wrapped in a towel
    and crushed with a rolling pin
1 small bay leaf, crumbled
2 cups white wine, preferably a
    Moselle
½ cup water
1 tablespoon flour

Preheat the oven to 325°. Line a roasting pan or casserole large enough to hold the fish comfortably with a wide strip of heavy-duty foil and let 2 inches extend over the pan at each end. With a pastry brush coat the foil lightly with 1 tablespoon of the soft butter.

Wash the fish under running water and dry it thoroughly with paper towels. Sprinkle it inside and out with salt and lemon juice. With a small, sharp knife, cut away a 1-inch-wide strip of skin from the backbone, starting just behind the head and reaching almost to the tail of the fish. Insert the potato into the cavity of the fish, then place the fish, split side down, in the lined pan. (The potato will serve to keep the back of the fish upright, but it is not meant to be served.) Lay the bacon strips over the exposed strip of flesh on the back, and sprinkle the fish lightly with white pepper. Pour the ¼ pound of melted butter over the entire surface of the fish and scatter the onions, allspice, cloves, peppercorns and bay leaf on top. Pour in 2 cups of wine and ½ cup of water and bring it to a boil over high heat. Cover the pan and bake in the middle of the oven for 30 to 40 minutes, or until the fish is firm when pressed lightly with a finger. Baste the fish once or twice with the pan liquids during the cooking process. Remove the pan from the oven, and using the long ends of foil as handles carefully lift out the fish. Gently slide it from the foil onto a large heated platter. Remove and discard the bacon strips and cover the fish loosely with foil to keep it warm while you make the sauce. Strain the liquid left in the pan through a fine sieve into a small saucepan, and bring to a boil over high heat. Continue to boil, uncovered, until the liquid is reduced to 1 cup, then reduce the heat to a simmer. In a small bowl, make a paste of the remaining 1 tablespoon of soft butter and a tablespoon of flour, and stir it bit by bit into the simmering liquid. Cook, stirring constantly, for 5 minutes, or until the sauce thickens slightly. Taste for seasoning and pour the sauce into a sauceboat. Serve separately with the fish. Remove the potato before you carve the fish.

Rollmöpse
ROLLMOPS

To serve 6 to 8

12 salt herring fillets, preferably *Matjes* herring
2 cups cider vinegar
2 cups cold water
3 juniper berries, 3 whole allspice, 3 whole cloves and 6 whole black peppercorns, bruised with a mortar and pestle or wrapped in a towel and bruised with a rolling pin

1 small bay leaf
¼ cup Düsseldorf-style prepared mustard, or substitute other hot prepared mustard
2 tablespoons capers, drained
3 medium-sized onions, peeled, thinly sliced and separated into rings
3 large dill pickles
Parsley sprigs

Place the herring fillets in a bowl and pour in enough water to cover them by about 1 inch. Soak them for at least 12 hours in the refrigerator, changing the water once or twice. Drain them well, rinse under cold running water and pat them dry with paper towels. Remove and discard any bones.

For the marinade, combine the vinegar, water, juniper berries, allspice, cloves, peppercorns and bay leaf in a 2- to 3-quart saucepan and bring them to a boil over high heat. Reduce the heat to low and simmer uncovered for 5 minutes. Then cool to room temperature.

Lay the herring fillets, skin side down, on a board or table. Spread 1 teaspoon of mustard evenly on each fillet and scatter ½ teaspoon of capers and several onion rings over the mustard. Cut the dill pickles lengthwise into quarters; if they are much longer than the width of the herring fillets, cut them crosswise into halves. Place a wedge of pickle at one narrow end of each of the fillets, and then roll the fillets jelly-roll fashion around the pickle into small, thick cylinders. Skewer the rolls with 2 or 3 toothpicks to secure them. Pack the rolls flat on their sides in a 2-quart glass loaf dish in two layers with the remaining onion rings scattered between the layers and over the top. (Do not use a metal pan, for the fish may pick up a metallic flavor.) Pour the marinade over the herring, then cover the dish with foil or plastic wrap and refrigerate it for 5 or 6 days before serving.

Serve the rollmops as an hors d'oeuvre on individual plates or arrange them on a platter. In either case, garnish them with onion rings and parsley.

NOTE: If salt herring fillets are not available, substitute 12 bottled Bismarck herring fillets. Drain them well, wash them thoroughly under cold running water and pat dry with paper towels. Then proceed with the recipe.

Heilbutt unterm Sahneberg
HALIBUT UNDER A MOUNTAIN OF CREAM

To serve 4

¼ cup dry white wine
¾ cup water
½ cup coarsely chopped onions
4 parsley sprigs
1 small bay leaf
6 whole black peppercorns
6 or 8 strips of lean bacon, about
    8 inches long
2 tablespoons finely chopped onions
4 tablespoons butter, softened

2 pounds halibut fillets, cut into
    serving pieces, or substitute 2
    pounds fillets of any other firm,
    white fish
½ teaspoon salt
1 tablespoon flour
1 teaspoon fresh lemon juice
⅛ teaspoon paprika
½ cup heavy cream
¼ cup freshly grated Parmesan
    cheese

In a heavy 1- to 1½-quart enameled or stainless-steel saucepan, bring the wine, water, ½ cup coarsely chopped onions, parsley, bay leaf and peppercorns to a boil over high heat. Reduce the heat to low and simmer, partially uncovered, for 20 minutes. Remove from the heat and set aside.

In a heavy 10- to 12-inch skillet, cook the bacon over moderate heat until it is lightly browned but still limp. With kitchen tongs, transfer the bacon to a double thickness of paper towels to drain. Pour off all but a tablespoon of fat from the skillet, add 2 tablespoons of finely chopped onions and cook over moderate heat, stirring frequently, for 5 minutes, or until the onions are soft and transparent but not brown.

Preheat the oven to 325°. Coat the bottom and sides of a shallow ovenproof serving dish large enough to hold the fish fillets in one layer with 2 tablespoons of the soft butter. Lay the fillets side by side in the bottom of the dish, and sprinkle them with ½ teaspoon of salt. Sprinkle the sautéed onions over the fish and lay the bacon strips on top. Strain the wine mixture over the fish, pressing down hard on the onions and herbs with the back of a spoon before discarding them. Bake the halibut in the middle of the oven for 12 to 15 minutes, or until the fish is firm and opaque. Discard the bacon and pour the cooking liquid through a fine sieve into a bowl. Cover the fish and set it aside in the baking dish.

To make the sauce, measure the strained cooking liquid and pour it into a small saucepan. If there is more than ½ cup, boil it briskly over high heat until it is reduced to that amount; if there is less, add more wine.

Bring the liquid to a boil over moderate heat. In a small bowl, make a paste of the remaining 2 tablespoons of butter and the flour, and when the mixture is smooth add it bit by bit to the poaching liquid. Reduce the heat and simmer, stirring constantly, for 5 minutes, or until the sauce thickens slightly. Remove the pan from the heat, and stir in the lemon juice and paprika. Taste for seasoning.

With a whisk or a rotary or electric beater, whip the cream in a chilled bowl until it forms firm peaks on the beater when it is lifted out of the bowl. Fold the cream gently into the sauce. Then, working quickly, pour the sauce over the fish and sprinkle the top with grated cheese. Slide the casserole under the broiler about 4 inches from the heat and broil for 1 or 2 minutes, or until the cheese melts and the sauce browns lightly. Serve at once, directly from the casserole.

Katerfisch
"FISH FOR A HANGOVER" WITH TOMATO SAUCE AND PICKLES

To serve 4

4 tablespoons butter
2 pounds gray, lemon or petrale
sole fillets or 2 pounds flounder
fillets, cut into serving pieces
2 tablespoons fresh lemon juice
½ teaspoon salt
2 medium-sized onions, peeled, thinly
sliced and separated into rings

3 tablespoons tomato purée
1 tablespoon white wine vinegar or
cider vinegar
½ teaspoon grated fresh horseradish
or 1 teaspoon bottled horseradish,
thoroughly drained and squeezed
dry in a towel
2 medium-sized dill pickles, cut
lengthwise into thin wedges

Preheat the oven to 375°. With 1 tablespoon of the butter, coat the bottom and sides of a shallow baking dish or casserole large enough to hold the fish in a single layer. Set the dish aside. Spread the fillets on wax paper, sprinkle them with lemon juice and salt, and let the fillets marinate for 10 minutes. In a heavy 8- to 10-inch skillet, melt 2 tablespoons of butter over moderate heat. When the foam subsides, drop in the onion rings and cook them, turning them frequently, for 5 minutes, or until the rings are soft and transparent but not brown.

Arrange the fish fillets side by side in the prepared baking dish. Beat the tomato purée, vinegar and horseradish together in a bowl, and spread the mixture evenly over the fillets. Scatter the onion rings and pickle wedges over the fish. Cut the remaining 1 tablespoon of butter into small pieces and dot the fish with them. Bake in the middle of the oven for about 15 minutes, or until the fillets are opaque and firm to the touch. Do not overcook. Serve at once, directly from the baking dish.

Meat and Poultry

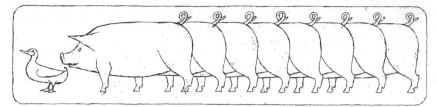

Westfälischer Pfefferpotthast
BEEF SHORT RIBS WITH SPICED LEMON-AND-CAPER SAUCE

To serve 4

2 pounds beef short ribs, cut into
  2-inch pieces
Salt
Freshly ground black pepper
2 tablespoons lard
6 medium-sized onions (about 2
  pounds), sliced ⅛ inch thick
1 small bay leaf

¼ teaspoon ground cloves
4 cups cold water
3 tablespoons fresh rye bread
  crumbs, made in a blender from
  1 slice fresh dark rye bread
2 teaspoons capers, drained and
  rinsed in cold water
2 tablespoons fresh lemon juice
½ teaspoon finely grated fresh
  lemon peel

Sprinkle the short ribs with salt and pepper. In a 3- to 4-quart flameproof casserole or Dutch oven, heat the lard over high heat, until it begins to splutter. Add the short ribs and brown them on all sides, regulating the heat so that the ribs brown quickly and evenly without burning. Remove the meat to a platter. Add the onions to the fat remaining in the casserole, and cook, stirring occasionally, for 5 minutes, or until they are soft and transparent but not brown. Add the bay leaf and cloves and pour in the water. Bring to a boil over high heat, scraping in any brown bits clinging to the bottom and sides of the pan.

Return the ribs to the casserole, cover and reduce the heat to its lowest point. Simmer for 1½ hours, or until the meat shows no resistance when pierced with the tip of a small, sharp knife. Then transfer the short ribs to a deep heated platter and cover with foil to keep them warm. Discard the bay leaf, and skim off the fat from the liquid remaining in the casserole. Stir in the bread crumbs, capers, lemon juice and lemon peel, and bring to a boil over high heat. Reduce the heat; simmer uncovered, for a minute or two. Taste for seasoning. The sauce should be quite peppery; add more pepper to taste if necessary. Then pour the sauce over the meat and serve at once.

Rouladen

BRAISED STUFFED BEEF ROLLS

To serve 6

3 pounds top round steak, sliced
½ inch thick, trimmed of all fat,
and pounded ¼ inch thick
6 teaspoons Düsseldorf-style
prepared mustard, or substitute
6 teaspoons other hot prepared
mustard
¼ cup finely chopped onions
6 slices lean bacon, each about
8 inches long
3 dill pickles, rinsed in cold water
and cut lengthwise into halves
3 tablespoons lard
2 cups water
1 cup coarsely chopped celery
¼ cup thinly sliced leeks, white
part only
1 tablespoon finely chopped scraped
parsnip
3 parsley sprigs
1 teaspoon salt
1 tablespoon butter
2 tablespoons flour

Cut the steak into 6 rectangular pieces about 4 inches wide and 8 inches long. Spread each rectangle with a teaspoon of mustard, sprinkle it with 2 teaspoons of onions, and place a slice of bacon down the center. Lay a strip of pickle across the narrow end of each piece and roll the meat around it, jelly-roll fashion, into a cylinder. Tie the rolls at each end with kitchen cord.

In a heavy 10- to 12-inch skillet melt the lard over moderate heat until it begins to splutter. Add the beef rolls, and brown them on all sides, regulating the heat so they color quickly and evenly without burning. Transfer the rolls to a plate, pour the water into the skillet and bring it to a boil, meanwhile scraping in any brown particles clinging to the bottom and sides of the pan. Add the celery, leeks, parsnip, parsley and salt, and return the beef rolls to the skillet. Cover, reduce the heat to low, and simmer for 1 hour, or until the meat shows no resistance when pierced with a fork. Turn the rolls once or twice during the cooking period. Transfer the rolls to a heated platter, and cover with foil to keep them warm while you make the sauce.

Strain the cooking liquid left in the skillet through a fine sieve, pressing down hard on the vegetables before discarding them. Measure the liquid, return it to the skillet, and boil briskly until it is reduced to 2 cups. Remove from the heat. Melt the butter in a small saucepan over moderate heat and, when the foam subsides, sprinkle in the flour. Lower the heat and cook, stirring constantly, until the flour turns a golden brown. Be careful not to let it burn. Gradually add the reduced cooking liquid, beating vigorously with a whisk until the sauce is smooth and thick. Taste for seasoning and return the sauce and the *Rouladen* to the skillet. Simmer over low heat only long enough to heat the rolls through. Serve the rolls on a heated platter and pour the sauce over them. *Rouladen* are often accompanied by red cabbage (*page 63*) and dumplings or boiled potatoes.

Königsberger Klopse
POACHED MEATBALLS IN LEMON-AND-CAPER SAUCE

To serve 4

MEATBALLS

1 tablespoon butter

½ cup finely chopped onions

2 slices homemade-type fresh white
    bread with crusts removed

2 tablespoons heavy cream

⅓ pound lean boneless beef, ⅓
    pound lean boneless pork, and ⅓
    pound lean boneless veal, ground

together 3 times

3 flat anchovy fillets, drained, rinsed
    in cold water and coarsely
    chopped, or substitute 1 teaspoon
    anchovy paste

2 tablespoons finely chopped parsley

2 eggs

½ teaspoon finely grated lemon peel

½ teaspoon salt

¼ teaspoon freshly ground black pepper

Melt 1 tablespoon of butter in a small skillet over moderate heat and in it cook the chopped onions for 5 minutes, or until they are transparent but not brown. Remove the skillet from the heat. Tear the bread into small pieces into a large bowl, add the cream and mix well. Add the onions, ground meat, anchovy fillets or anchovy paste, parsley, eggs, lemon peel, ½ teaspoon salt and black pepper. Knead vigorously with both hands until the ingredients are well combined, then put the mixture through the finest blade of a meat grinder. Moistening your hands lightly with cold water, shape the mixture into 8 large meatballs about 2 inches in diameter.

POACHING LIQUID

2 quarts water

1 medium-sized onion, peeled and

pierced with 1 whole clove

1 small bay leaf

1 teaspoon salt

In a heavy 6- to 8-quart saucepan or soup pot, bring the water, whole onion, bay leaf and 1 teaspoon of salt to a boil over high heat. Boil, uncovered, for 10 minutes. Then reduce the heat to low and drop in the meatballs. Simmer, uncovered, for 20 minutes, or until the *Klopse* rise to the surface of the water. With a slotted spoon, transfer them to a deep heated platter and cover them with aluminum foil to prevent their darkening upon exposure to air. Strain the poaching liquid through a fine sieve into a bowl and put it aside.

SAUCE

4 tablespoons butter

4 tablespoons flour

3 tablespoons fresh lemon juice

1 tablespoon capers, drained

2 egg yolks

2 tablespoons sour cream

In a heavy 10- to 12-inch skillet, melt 4 tablespoons of butter over moderate heat. When the foam subsides, stir in the flour. Pour in 3 cups of the poaching liquid and bring it to a boil, beating constantly with a whisk until the sauce thickens and is smooth. Reduce the heat to low, add the lemon juice and capers and simmer uncovered, stirring occasionally, for 15 minutes. In a small bowl break the egg yolks up with a fork, then stir into them ¼ cup of the simmering sauce. Whisk the mixture back into the skillet and stir in the sour cream. Taste for seasoning. Add the meatballs and simmer, basting from time to time, until they are thoroughly heated. To serve, return the meatballs to the platter, and pour the sauce over them.

Rindfleisch mit Schnittlauchsosse
BOILED BEEF WITH CHIVE SAUCE

To serve 4 to 6

3 pounds lean boneless beef chuck
  or lean brisket of beef
2 medium-sized carrots, scraped
2 celery stalks, with their leaves
1 leek, white part only
1 large onion, peeled
4 parsley sprigs

5 whole black peppercorns
2 teaspoons salt
4 tablespoons butter
3 tablespoons flour
½ cup light cream
¼ cup finely chopped fresh chives,
  or substitute ¼ cup green scallion
  tops, finely chopped
¼ teaspoon ground nutmeg

Place the beef in a heavy 4- to 5-quart flameproof casserole or Dutch oven, and pour in enough water to cover the beef by about 2 inches. Bring to a boil over high heat, meanwhile skimming off any scum that rises to the surface. Add the carrots, celery stalks, leek, onion, parsley sprigs, peppercorns and salt, then reduce the heat to its lowest point, partially cover the casserole, and simmer for 2½ to 3 hours, or until the meat shows no resistance when pierced with a fork. Transfer the meat to a heated plate and cover it with aluminum foil to keep it warm. Strain the cooking stock into a bowl and discard the vegetables. Skim as much of the surface fat from the stock as you can.

In a heavy 8- to 10-inch skillet, melt the butter over moderate heat, and when the foam subsides, add the flour. Stirring constantly, cook the mixture for 1 or 2 minutes. Do not let the flour brown. Slowly pour in 2 cups of the strained stock and then the cream. Bring the sauce to a boil, beating constantly with a whisk until it is thick and smooth. Reduce the heat to low and simmer for 10 minutes. Add the chives and nutmeg and taste for seasoning. If the sauce is too thick for your taste, thin with a few tablespoons of the reserved stock.

To serve, carve the meat into thin slices and arrange them slightly overlapping on a large, heated platter. Spoon a few tablespoons of the sauce over the meat and pass the rest separately in a sauceboat.

Sauerbraten

MARINATED POT ROAST IN SWEET-AND-SOUR SAUCE

To serve 6 to 8

½ cup dry red wine
½ cup red wine vinegar
2 cups cold water
1 medium-sized onion, peeled and
    thinly sliced
5 black peppercorns and 4 whole
    juniper berries coarsely crushed
    with a mortar and pestle
2 small bay leaves
1 teaspoon salt
4 pounds boneless beef roast,
    preferably top or bottom round

or rump, trimmed of fat
3 tablespoons lard
½ cup finely chopped onions
½ cup finely chopped carrots
¼ cup finely chopped celery
2 tablespoons flour
½ cup water
½ cup gingersnap crumbs, or 1 cup
    crumbled honey cake made from
    the recipe on page 88, or 1 cup
    crumbled ready-made imported
    honey cake

In a 2- to 3-quart saucepan, combine the wine, vinegar, water, sliced onion, crushed peppercorns and juniper berries, bay leaves and salt. Bring this marinade to a boil over high heat, then remove it from the heat and let it cool to room temperature. Place the beef in a deep crock or a deep stainless-steel or enameled pot just large enough to hold it comfortably and pour the marinade over it. The marinade should come at least halfway up the sides of the meat; if necessary, add more wine. Turn the meat in the marinade to moisten it on all sides. Then cover the pan tightly with foil or plastic wrap and refrigerate for 2 to 3 days, turning the meat over at least twice a day.

Remove the meat from the marinade and pat it completely dry with paper towels. Strain the marinade through a fine sieve set over a bowl and reserve the liquid. Discard the spices and onions.

In a heavy 5-quart flameproof casserole, melt the lard over high heat until it begins to splutter. Add the meat and brown it on all sides, turning it frequently and regulating the heat so that it browns deeply and evenly without burning. This should take about 15 minutes. Transfer the meat to a platter, and pour off and discard all but about 2 tablespoons of the fat from the casserole. Add the chopped onions, carrots and celery to the fat in the casserole and cook them over moderate heat, stirring frequently, for 5 to 8 minutes, or until they are soft and light brown. Sprinkle 2 tablespoons of flour over the vegetables and cook, stirring constantly, for 2 or 3 minutes longer, or until the flour begins to color. Pour in 2 cups of the reserved marinade and ½ cup of water and bring to a boil over high heat. Return the meat to the casserole. Cover tightly and simmer over low heat for 2 hours, or until the meat shows no resistance when pierced with the tip of a sharp knife. Transfer the meat to a heated platter and cover it with aluminum foil to keep it warm while you make the sauce.

Pour the liquid left in the casserole into a large measuring cup and skim the fat from the surface. You will need 2½ cups of liquid for the sauce. If you have more, boil it briskly over high heat until it is reduced to that amount; if you have less, add some of the reserved marinade. Combine the liquid and the gingersnap or honey-cake crumbs in a small saucepan, and cook over moderate heat, stirring frequently, for 10 minutes. The crumbs will disintegrate in the sauce and thicken it slightly. Strain the sauce through a fine sieve, pressing down hard with a wooden spoon to force as much of the vegetables and crumbs through as possible. Return the sauce to the pan, taste for seasoning and let it simmer over a low heat until ready to serve.

To serve, carve the meat into ¼-inch-thick slices and arrange the slices attractively in overlapping layers on a heated platter. Moisten the slices with a few tablespoons of the sauce and pass the remaining sauce separately in a sauceboat. Traditionally, *Sauerbraten* is served with dumplings or boiled potatoes and red cabbage *(page 63)*.

NOTE: If you prefer, you may cook the *Sauerbraten* in the oven rather than on top of the stove. Bring the casserole to a boil over high heat, cover tightly and cook in a preheated 350° oven for about 2 hours.

Beefsteak Tartar

BEEFSTEAK TARTAR

To serve 2

½ pound lean boneless beef, preferably beef tenderloin, or top or eye round, ground 2 or 3 times
2 egg yolks
2 tablespoons salt
2 tablespoons freshly ground black pepper

2 tablespoons capers, thoroughly drained
2 tablespoons finely chopped onions
2 tablespoons finely chopped fresh parsley
8 flat anchovy fillets, thoroughly drained
Dark bread
Butter

Traditionally the beef for beefsteak Tartar is ground very fine and served as soon as possible thereafter. Shape the beef into two mounds and place them in the center of separate serving plates. Make a well in the middle of the mounds and carefully drop an egg yolk in each.

Serve the salt, black pepper, capers, chopped onions, parsley and anchovy fillets in small separate saucers. The beef and other ingredients are then combined at the table to individual taste. Serve beefsteak Tartar with dark bread and butter.

Würzfleisch
BEEF IN SPICED SOUR-CREAM SAUCE

To serve 4

4 tablespoons flour
1 teaspoon salt
½ teaspoon freshly ground black
  pepper
2 pounds top round steak, sliced ½
  inch thick and cut into 4 pieces
3 tablespoons lard

½ cup finely chopped onions
1 teaspoon paprika
6 whole black peppercorns
3 whole allspice
½ small bay leaf
1 whole clove
2 cups water
1 cup sour cream
1 tablespoon Madeira

In a mixing bowl, combine 3 tablespoons of the flour with the salt and pepper. Dip the pieces of beef in the seasoned flour one at a time, then vigorously shake off the excess. In a heavy 10- to 12-inch skillet, melt 2 tablespoons of the lard over high heat until a light haze forms above it. Add the beef and brown it on both sides, regulating the heat so the meat browns quickly and evenly without burning. Remove the meat to a platter and add the remaining tablespoon of lard to the skillet. Then drop in the onions and cook over moderate heat, stirring occasionally, for 5 to 8 minutes, or until the onions are soft and slightly brown. Add the paprika, peppercorns, allspice, bay leaf and clove. Pour in the water and bring it to a boil, meanwhile scraping into it any brown sediment clinging to the bottom and sides of the skillet.

Return the meat to the pan, reduce the heat to low, and cover tightly. Simmer for 1½ to 2 hours, basting the meat occasionally with its cooking liquid. When the beef can easily be pierced with the tip of a fork, transfer it to a plate and cover with aluminum foil to keep it warm.

Strain the cooking liquid through a fine sieve into a small bowl, pressing down hard on the onions with the back of a spoon before discarding them. There should be 1½ to 2 cups of liquid in the bowl. If there is less than that amount add canned or fresh beef stock; if more, boil the liquid briskly over high heat until it is reduced to 2 cups. Return the liquid to the skillet, bring to a simmer over high heat, then reduce the heat to low. With a whisk, beat the remaining tablespoon of flour into the sour cream. A few tablespoons at a time, beat the sour cream into the simmering liquid and cook, whisking constantly, until the sauce is hot and slightly thickened. Do not let it boil. Return the beef to the skillet, baste it well with the sauce, and cook just long enough to heat it through. Stir in the Madeira and taste for seasoning. To serve, arrange the meat on a heated platter. Moisten the slices with a few tablespoons of sauce and serve the rest separately in a sauceboat. Traditionally, *Würzfleisch* is accompanied by dumplings or boiled or mashed potatoes.

Kalbshaxe mit Gewürzgurkensosse

VEAL SHANKS IN PICKLE SAUCE

To serve 4 to 6

2 meaty veal shanks (about 4 to 5 pounds), each sawed into 2 or 3 pieces
1 medium-sized onion peeled and cut into 1/4-inch slices
1 carrot, scraped and cut into 1/4-inch slices

1 leek, white part only, thoroughly washed and cut into 1/8-inch slices
2 parsley sprigs
2 tablespoons cider vinegar
1 whole clove
1 small bay leaf
3 whole black peppercorns
1 teaspoon salt

In a heavy 8-quart casserole or soup pot, combine the veal shanks, onion, carrot, leek, parsley, vinegar, clove, bay leaf, peppercorns, and 1 teaspoon salt. Pour in enough water to just cover the shanks. Bring to a boil over high heat, skimming off the foam and scum that rise to the surface. Reduce the heat to its lowest point, cover the casserole, and simmer for 1 hour, or until the meat shows no resistance when pierced with the tip of a small, sharp knife. With tongs, transfer the shanks to a plate. Strain the cooking stock through a fine sieve set over a large bowl, skim off all fat and set the stock aside. When the veal shanks are cool enough to handle, trim off the fat with a small knife and cut the meat away from the bones. Discard the bones, and cut the meat into 1-inch pieces.

SAUCE

4 tablespoons butter
1/2 cup finely chopped onions
3 tablespoons flour

1 cup finely chopped dill pickle
1/2 teaspoon salt
Freshly ground black pepper

In a heavy 10- to 12-inch skillet, melt the butter over moderate heat. When the foam subsides, add 1/2 cup of the chopped onions and cook, stirring frequently for 5 minutes, or until they are soft and transparent but not brown. Stir in the flour and cook for another minute or so. Gradually pour in 3 cups of the reserved stock, stirring constantly with a whisk until the sauce is lightly thickened and smooth. Add the chopped pickle, 1/2 teaspoon salt and a few grindings of pepper, and simmer, uncovered, for 10 minutes, stirring occasionally. Then add the veal and simmer for another 5 minutes, or only long enough to heat it through. Serve at once from a deep, heated platter or serving bowl.

Ragoût Fin

VEAL TONGUE, SWEETBREADS AND MUSHROOMS IN WHITE WINE SAUCE

To serve 6 as a first course

TONGUE

A 1-pound fresh veal tongue
1 cup coarsely chopped onions
½ cup coarsely chopped leeks, including 2 inches of the green tops
½ cup coarsely chopped celery with leaves

¼ cup coarsely chopped, scraped parsnip
2 sprigs parsley
6 peppercorns
3 whole allspice
1 whole clove
1 teaspoon salt

TONGUE: In a pot large enough to hold all the vegetables comfortably, combine the tongue, chopped onions, leeks, celery, parsnip, parsley, peppercorns, allspice, clove and salt. Pour in enough cold water to cover the tongue by at least 2 inches and bring to a boil over high heat. Then reduce the heat to low, partially cover the pot and simmer for about 2 hours, or until the meat shows no resistance when pierced with the tip of a sharp knife. Add boiling water to the pot if needed; the tongue should be covered with water throughout the cooking period. Remove the tongue from the stock, and while it is still hot, skin it with a small, sharp knife, cutting away the fat, bones and gristle at its base. Cut the meat into ¼-inch dice and set aside. Discard the cooking liquid and vegetables.

SWEETBREADS
1 pair veal sweetbreads (about ¾ pound)

Distilled white vinegar
1 teaspoon lemon juice
2 teaspoons salt

SWEETBREADS: Soak the sweetbreads in enough cold water to cover them, for 2 hours, changing the water every 30 minutes or so; then soak them for another hour in acidulated cold water, using 1 tablespoon of vinegar for each quart of water. Gently pull off as much of the outside membrane as possible without tearing the sweetbreads. Cut the two lobes of the pair of sweetbreads from the tube between them with a small, sharp knife; discard the tube. Place the sweetbreads in an enameled saucepan with enough water to cover them by 2 inches, add the 1 teaspoon lemon juice and 2 teaspoons salt and bring to a boil. Reduce the heat to its lowest point and simmer uncovered for 15 to 20 minutes, or until the sweetbreads are tender but still firm. Drain and pat them dry with paper towels. Then cut them into ¼-inch dice and set them aside.

MUSHROOMS   1 teaspoon salt
8 large fresh mushrooms   1 teaspoon fresh lemon juice

MUSHROOMS: Wipe the mushrooms with a damp paper towel and cut away the tough ends of the stems. Bring 3 cups of water, 1 teaspoon salt and 1 teaspoon of lemon juice to a boil in a 2- to 3-quart enameled or stainless-steel saucepan and drop in the mushrooms. Reduce the heat to low, cover, and simmer for about 4 minutes. Drain the mushrooms thoroughly and cut them into ¼-inch dice. Set them aside.

SAUCE
3 tablespoons butter   ¼ cup dry white wine
4 tablespoons flour   2 egg yolks
1¾ cups chicken stock, fresh or   2 teaspoons lemon juice
    canned   ⅛ teaspoon white pepper

SAUCE: In a 2-quart enameled or stainless-steel saucepan, melt 3 table-spoons of butter over moderate heat. When the foam subsides, stir in the flour. Pour in the chicken stock and wine and, beating vigorously with a whisk, bring the sauce to a boil. When it is quite thick and smooth, reduce the heat to low and simmer slowly for 2 to 3 minutes. Break up the egg yolks with a fork and stir in ¼ cup of the simmering sauce. Whisk the mixture back into the pan and bring the sauce to a boil, stirring constantly. Boil for 30 seconds, remove from the heat and stir in the lemon juice and pepper. Taste for seasoning.

1 tablespoon capers, drained and
    rinsed in cold water   ¼ cup freshly grated Parmesan
¼ cup dry bread crumbs   cheese

TO ASSEMBLE: Preheat the oven to 450°. In a large bowl combine the sauce, reserved tongue, sweetbreads and mushrooms but do not include any juices that may have accumulated around them. With a large spoon mix together gently but thoroughly and taste for seasoning. Divide the mixture evenly among 6 small buttered scallop shells. Spread the top with the capers, then sprinkle the bread crumbs and grated cheese over them. Bake in the middle of the oven for 10 to 15 minutes, or until the sauce bubbles and the top browns lightly. For a crustier surface, slide the shells under a hot broiler for a few seconds, watching carefully to prevent the top from burning. Serve at once.

NOTE: *Ragoût fin* is also often served as a luncheon dish. For this purpose, the sauce, tongue, sweetbreads and mushrooms are combined and reheated briefly in a saucepan, then spooned into 6 patty shells and served without the final garniture of capers, crumbs and cheese.

Kalbsrolle
BRAISED STUFFED VEAL ROLL

To serve 6 to 8

POACHING STOCK

The bones from a leg or breast of
  veal, sawed into 2-inch lengths
4 cups water

½ cup coarsely chopped onions
½ cup coarsely chopped celery,
  including the leaves
6 whole black peppercorns
1 small bay leaf

In a heavy 3- to 4-quart saucepan, bring the veal bones and water to a boil over high heat, skimming off any foam and scum that rise to the surface. Add the ½ cup of coarsely chopped onions, the celery, peppercorns and bay leaf, reduce the heat to low and partially cover the pan. Simmer, undisturbed, for 1 hour. Strain the stock through a fine sieve set over a bowl, discarding the bones, vegetables and spices. Set the stock aside.

STUFFING

2 slices homemade type fresh white
  bread
⅓ cup milk
1 tablespoon butter
½ cup finely chopped onions
½ pound ground beef chuck
½ pound fresh sausage meat
1 egg, lightly beaten

3 tablespoons finely chopped parsley
⅛ teaspoon ground nutmeg
Salt
Freshly ground black pepper

A 4- to 4½-pound breast of veal,
  boned and trimmed
3 tablespoons lard

Tear the slices of bread into small pieces and soak them in the milk for 5 minutes, then gently squeeze them and set them aside in a large mixing bowl. In a small skillet, melt the butter over moderate heat. When the foam subsides add ½ cup of finely chopped onions and cook, stirring frequently, for 5 minutes, or until they are soft and transparent but not brown. With a rubber spatula, scrape the contents of the skillet into the bowl with the bread, and add the beef, sausage meat, egg, parsley, nutmeg, ¼ teaspoon of salt and a few grindings of pepper. Knead the mixture with your hands or beat with a large spoon until all the ingredients are well blended.

Preheat the oven to 325°. Place the boned veal flat side down on a board or table, sprinkle it with salt and a few grindings of pepper and, with a knife or spatula, spread the ground-meat stuffing mixture evenly over the veal. Beginning with a wide side, roll up the veal jelly-roll fashion into a thick cylinder. Tie the roll at both ends and in the center with 8-inch lengths of white kitchen cord.

In a heavy flameproof casserole just large enough to hold the roll comfortably, melt the lard over high heat until a light haze forms above it. Add the veal roll and brown it on all sides, regulating the heat so that it browns quickly and evenly without burning. Pour in the reserved stock and bring it to a boil over high heat.

Cover the casserole and transfer it to the middle of the oven. Cook for 1¾ hours, turning the roll over after the first hour. Then remove the cover and cook, basting occasionally with the pan juices, for 30 minutes longer, or until the veal is tender and shows no resistance when pierced with the tip of a small, sharp knife.

To serve hot, carve the veal into ¼-inch slices and arrange them attractively in overlapping layers on a heated platter. Skim and discard the fat from the juices in the casserole, taste for seasoning, and either pour over the veal or serve separately in a sauceboat. (If you would like to make a sauce, measure the skimmed juices. If there is more than 2 cups, boil briskly to reduce it; if there is less, add water. Melt 2 tablespoons of butter over moderate heat and, when the foam subsides, stir in 3 tablespoons of flour. Cook, stirring, over low heat until the flour browns lightly. Gradually add the pan juices, beating vigorously with a whisk until the sauce is smooth and thick. Taste for seasoning.)

To serve cold, transfer the veal roll to a loaf pan and pour the degreased cooking juices over it. Cool to room temperature, then refrigerate overnight. When cold, the juices should jell into a light aspic. Serve the veal cut into thin slices.

Traditionally, *Kalbsrolle* is accompanied by plain boiled potatoes and a selection of boiled or braised vegetables such as peas, leeks, cauliflower, green beans and carrots.

Kalbsnierenbraten

VEAL ROAST STUFFED WITH KIDNEY

To serve 6 to 8

A 6- to 8-ounce veal kidney, peeled
   and trimmed of fat
Salt
Freshly ground black pepper
½ teaspoon dried thyme
A 5-pound loin roast of veal, boned,
   with some of the flank left on
4 tablespoons lard

½ cup finely chopped onions
½ cup finely chopped carrots
½ cup finely chopped celery (stalk
   only)
3 cups fresh beef or chicken stock,
   or 1½ cups canned beef or chicken
   stock combined with 1½ cups
   water
1 tablespoon cornstarch
3 tablespoons cold water

Ask your butcher to stuff the veal loin with the kidney, or do it yourself in the following fashion: With a small, sharp knife, split the kidney in half lengthwise and remove all the fat and membrane. Sprinkle the cut halves liberally with salt and a few grindings of pepper, and firmly press thyme into them. Spread the veal loin out flat, cut side up, and lay the kidney down the center, placing the halves end to end, and overlapping them slightly. Bring one side of the veal over the kidneys and roll the roast up, jelly-roll fashion, into a long thick cylinder. Tie it at both ends and in two or three places along its length with white kitchen cord. Coat the surface of the veal evenly with 2 tablespoons of lard, and sprinkle it lightly with salt and a few grindings of pepper.

Preheat the oven to 350°. In a heavy casserole or Dutch oven just large enough to hold the veal comfortably, melt the remaining 2 tablespoons of lard over high heat until it splutters. Reduce the heat to moderate and add the onions, carrots and celery. Cook, stirring frequently, for 5 minutes, or until the vegetables are soft but not brown. Then place the veal on top of the vegetables, pour in the stock and roast uncovered in the middle of the oven for about 1½ hours, or until it is tender and can easily be pierced with the tip of a small, sharp knife. Baste it every 15 minutes or so with the cooking juices in the casserole. Transfer the veal to a heated platter and let it rest for 10 minutes or so before carving.

Meanwhile make the sauce in the following fashion: Strain the casserole cooking juices through a fine sieve into a small bowl, pressing down hard on the vegetables with the back of a spoon before discarding them. Skim the fat from the surface. Measure the liquid and pour it into a small saucepan. If there is more than 2 cups, boil it briskly over high heat until reduced to the required amount; if there is less, add more stock. Dissolve the cornstarch in 3 tablespoons of cold water and pour it slowly into the pan, stirring constantly over moderate heat until the sauce thickens slightly and becomes clear. Taste for seasoning.

To serve, carve the veal into ¼-inch slices; each slice will have a round of kidney in the center. Arrange the slices attractively on a heated platter, overlapping them slightly. Moisten the slices with a few tablespoons of the sauce and serve the rest separately in a sauceboat.

Hammel Koteletten mit Zwiebelsosse
LAMB CHOPS IN ONION SAUCE

To serve 6

6 shoulder lamb chops, cut ½ inch
    thick and trimmed of excess fat
Salt
Freshly ground black pepper
4 tablespoons lard

2 tablespoons butter
1½ cups finely chopped onions
1 tablespoon flour
1½ cups heavy cream
⅛ teaspoon ground nutmeg
¼ pound boiled or baked smoked
    ham, chopped fine (about ½ cup)

Preheat the oven to 330°. Pat the chops completely dry with paper towels and sprinkle them generously on both sides with salt and pepper. In a heavy 12-inch skillet, melt the lard over high heat until a light haze forms above it. Add the chops and brown them well on each side, regulating the heat so that the meat colors quickly and evenly without burning. Transfer the chops to a shallow, flameproof casserole large enough to hold them in one layer.

Discard the fat in the skillet, and in its place add the 2 tablespoons of butter. Melt it over moderate heat, and when the foam subsides add the onions. Cook, stirring occasionally, for 8 to 10 minutes, or until the onions are soft, transparent and light brown. Stir in the flour, mix thoroughly, then gradually pour in the cream, stirring constantly with a whisk. Bring to a boil, continuing to stir until the sauce is smooth and thick. Add the nutmeg and taste for seasoning. Then purée the sauce through a coarse sieve set over a bowl, pressing down hard on the onions with the back of a spoon before discarding them, and stir the chopped ham into the sauce. Spoon the sauce over the lamb chops and bring to a simmer over moderate heat. Cover the casserole tightly and bake in the middle of the oven for 15 minutes, or until the chops are tender. Serve the chops directly from the casserole.

Piquante Hammelschulter
BRAISED LAMB SHOULDER WITH MUSTARD AND RED WINE SAUCE

To serve 6 to 8

LAMB

A 6-pound boned lamb shoulder, trimmed of all fat and outer skin removed (have the bones chopped into 3-inch lengths and keep them to make the stock)

⅓ cup Düsseldorf-style prepared mustard, or substitute ⅓ cup other hot prepared mustard
1 teaspoon salt
1 teaspoon paprika

Spread the lamb shoulder flat on a strip of wax paper and with a pastry brush spread the top side of the meat evenly with 4 tablespoons of mustard. Sprinkle it with ½ teaspoon of the salt and ½ teaspoon of the paprika, then roll it with the grain, jelly-roll fashion, into a compact cylinder. Tie the roll at both ends and in the center with 12-inch lengths of white kitchen cord. Place it in a deep dish large enough to hold it comfortably. Spread the outside of the roll with the remaining 2 tablespoons of mustard, and sprinkle it with the remaining ½ teaspoon of salt and ½ teaspoon of paprika. Drape a piece of wax paper loosely over the meat and let it rest in the refrigerator to absorb the mustard flavor for at least 24 hours and up to 3 to 4 days.

STOCK

Lamb shoulder bones
6 cups cold water
1 medium-sized onion, peeled, quartered and pierced with 2 cloves
1 carrot, scraped and cut into 2-inch pieces
A bouquet made of 4 parsley sprigs,

½ small bay leaf and 2 celery tops wrapped together in cheesecloth
2 tablespoons lard
1 large onion, cut into ⅛-inch slices and separated into rings
2 teaspoons cornstarch
1 tablespoon cold water
½ cup dry red wine

To make the stock, combine the bones and 6 cups of cold water in a heavy 4- to 5-quart saucepan. The water should cover the bones by 1 inch; add more if needed. Bring to a boil over high heat, skimming off any scum that rises to the surface. Then add the quartered onion, carrot and bouquet. Reduce the heat to low, partially cover the pan and simmer for 2 hours. Strain the stock into a bowl and discard the bones and vegetables. Then boil the strained stock briskly over high heat until it is reduced to 1 cup.

Preheat the oven to 350°. In a heavy casserole or Dutch oven just large enough to hold the meat comfortably, melt the lard over high heat until a light haze forms above it. Add the lamb and brown it lightly on all sides, regulating the heat so that the meat colors quickly and evenly without burning.

26

Remove the lamb to a platter. To the fat remaining in the pan, add the onion rings, and cook, stirring frequently, for 5 minutes, or until they are soft and lightly colored. Skim the fat from the reserved lamb stock and pour it into the casserole. Bring it to a boil, meanwhile scraping into it any brown bits clinging to the bottom or sides of the pan. Return the lamb to the casserole, cover, and bake in the middle of the oven for 1½ to 2 hours, basting it every 20 minutes or so. When the meat is tender, transfer it to the heated platter and cover it with the foil to keep warm.

Strain the juices remaining in the casserole through a fine sieve into a small saucepan, pressing down hard on the onion rings with the back of a spoon to extract their juices before discarding them. Skim the fat from the surface with a large spoon and bring the liquid to a simmer over moderate heat. Dissolve the cornstarch in the water and pour it slowly into the pan, stirring constantly. Simmer, stirring occasionally, for 2 or 3 minutes, or until the sauce thickens slightly and becomes clear. Add the red wine and simmer for 5 minutes longer. Taste for seasoning.

To serve, carve the meat into thin slices and arrange the slices in overlapping layers on a large, heated platter. Serve the sauce separately in a sauceboat.

NOTE: In Germany, this dish is traditionally made with *Hammelschulter,* or mutton shoulder. If your butcher is able to obtain mutton (or yearling) you may substitute it for the lamb in this recipe.

Sülzkoteletten

PORK CHOPS IN ASPIC

To serve 6

A 2-pound loin of pork, center cut,
  with the backbone (chine) sawed
  through but left attached and tied
  to the loin in 2 or 3 places
2 cups dry white wine
½ cup white wine vinegar
5½ cups cold water
1 medium-sized onion, peeled and
  pierced with 2 whole cloves
1 scraped carrot, cut into ¼-inch
  slices
2 celery stalks, including the leaves,
  coarsely chopped
10 parsley sprigs
1 bay leaf

1 teaspoon salt
¼ teaspoon freshly ground black
  pepper
2 envelopes unflavored gelatin
2 egg whites, beaten to a froth
Garnish as desired with thinly sliced
  and fancifully cut flowers made
  from any combination of cooked
  or raw carrots, drained and rinsed
  sweet gherkins, drained and rinsed
  pimientos, drained and rinsed
  pickled cauliflower, blanched
  scallion or leek tops, peeled
  cucumber, peeled and seeded
  tomato, and whites of hard-cooked
  eggs

In a deep, heavy casserole or a soup pot just large enough to hold the meat comfortably, combine the pork loin, wine, vinegar and 5 cups of cold water. Bring to a boil over high heat, meanwhile skimming off the foam and scum that rise to the surface. Reduce the heat to low and add the onion, carrot, celery, parsley, bay leaf, salt and pepper. Cover the casserole and simmer the pork for 1½ hours, or until it is tender and shows no resistance when pierced with the tip of a sharp knife.

Transfer the pork to a plate and let it cool to room temperature. Then cover it with aluminum foil or plastic wrap and refrigerate. (If you plan to use the carrot slices to garnish the chops in the finished dish, reserve them on the plate with the pork loin.)

Strain the cooking stock through a fine sieve into a large bowl, discarding the vegetables and herbs. With a large spoon skim the surface of all fat. There should be about 5 cups of stock. If more, boil briskly, uncovered, until reduced to the required amount.

Prepare the aspic in the following fashion: Sprinkle the gelatin into the ½ cup of cold water and let it soften for 5 minutes. Then, in a 3- to 4-quart saucepan, combine it with the stock and add the beaten egg whites. Over high heat, bring the stock to a boil, meanwhile stirring constantly with a whisk. When the stock begins to froth and rise, remove the pan from the heat. Let it rest for 5 minutes, then pour it into a large sieve lined with a damp kitchen towel and set over a large bowl. Allow the aspic to drain through without disturbing it at any point, then taste for seasoning (it will probably need more salt) and set it aside. Do not refrigerate.

Carefully carve the pork loin into 6 chops about ½ inch thick. Cut the meat and fat away from the bones and trim the chops into neat, symmetrical cutlets. Pour a layer about ⅛ inch thick of the aspic into each of 6 cutlet molds or into a shallow baking dish large enough to hold the cutlets comfortably in one layer. Chill in the refrigerator until firmly set. Decorate the surface of the set aspic with the garnish of your choice and carefully place the chops on top of it.

Pour enough liquid aspic into the mold or baking dish to come halfway up the sides of the chops and refrigerate again until the aspic is firm. (This step is necessary to prevent the chops from rising to the surface of the molds when the remaining aspic is added.) When the chops are firmly anchored, cover them completely with liquid aspic and refrigerate for at least 4 hours, until firm. Any remaining aspic may be chilled in a flat pan or dish at the same time and used chopped or cut into decorative shapes as a garnish when the chops are served.

To unmold chops from individual molds, run a small, sharp knife around the side of each mold, then dip the bottom into hot water for a few seconds. Wipe the mold dry and turn it out on a chilled serving plate.

The chops in the baking dish may be served directly from the dish or you may unmold them in the following fashion: Run a sharp knife around the sides of the dish and dip the bottom in hot water for a few seconds. Place a flat, shallow platter upside down over the dish and, grasping the platter and dish firmly together, invert them. Rap them on a table and the aspic should slide out easily.

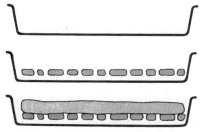

To make pork cutlets molded in aspic (*recipe above*), first pour a ⅛-inch film of liquid aspic into the mold and refrigerate until firm (*top*). Add the decorations (*center*). Now place a cutlet on top and pour in enough liquid aspic to cover it halfway. Refrigerate until set, and then fill the mold with aspic and refrigerate again (*bottom*). When all the layers are firm, the mold is ready to unmold and serve.

Schweinskoteletten mit Knackwurst und Kartoffeln
PORK CHOPS WITH KNOCKWURST AND POTATOES

To serve 6

1 tablespoon caraway seeds
½ teaspoon salt
¼ teaspoon freshly ground black
   pepper
6 center cut loin pork chops, cut ½
   inch thick
½ cup flour
2 tablespoons lard
½ pound knockwurst, sliced into ¼-
   inch rounds
1 cup coarsely chopped onions
½ cup coarsely chopped, scraped
   carrots

½ cup coarsely chopped celery
3 small sweet gherkins, drained,
   rinsed in cold water, and finely
   chopped
1 cup chicken stock, fresh or canned
4 large boiling potatoes (about 1½
   pounds), peeled and sliced into ⅛-
   inch rounds
6 medium-sized tomatoes, peeled,
   seeded and coarsely chopped, or
   substitute 2 cups drained, canned
   whole-pack tomatoes

Combine the caraway seeds, salt and pepper, and press the mixture firmly into both sides of the pork chops. Dip the chops in flour, then shake off the excess. In a heavy 12-inch skillet melt the lard over high heat until a light haze forms above it. Brown the chops for about 5 minutes on each side, turning them with kitchen tongs and regulating the heat so that the meat colors quickly and evenly without burning. Transfer the chops to a plate and add the knockwurst, onions, carrots, celery and gherkins to the fat remaining in the skillet. Cook over moderate heat, stirring frequently, for 5 minutes. Return the chops to the pan and pour in the stock. The stock should come just to the top of the chops without covering them. If necessary add more stock or water. Arrange the potato slices evenly over the chops, covering them completely and scatter the chopped tomatoes over them. Bring to a boil over high heat, reduce the heat to low, and cover the skillet. Simmer undisturbed for 45 minutes, or until the potatoes and chops show no resistance when pierced with the tip of a sharp knife. Serve directly from the skillet.

Kasseler Rippenspeer
ROASTED SMOKED PORK LOIN

To serve 4 to 6

2 tablespoons lard
1 cup coarsely chopped onions
1 cup coarsely chopped carrots
A 3½ to 4 pound smoked pork
  loin in one piece, with the
  backbone (chine) sawed
  through at ½-inch intervals, but

left attached and tied to the
  loin in 2 or 3 places
4 whole juniper berries, coarsely
  crushed with a mortar and pestle
  or wrapped in a towel and
  crushed with a rolling pin
4 cups cold water
2 teaspoons cornstarch dissolved
  in 1 tablespoon cold water

Preheat the oven to 350°. In a heavy 8- to 10-inch skillet, melt the lard over moderate heat. Add the onions and carrots and cook over moderate heat, stirring frequently for 8 to 10 minutes, or until the vegetables are soft and light brown. With a rubber spatula, scrape the entire contents of the skillet into a heavy casserole or roasting pan just large enough to hold the pork comfortably. Place the pork loin, fat side up, on top of the vegetables and strew the crushed juniper berries around the pork. Pour in the 4 cups of water and roast uncovered in the middle of the oven, basting occasionally with the cooking juices, for 1½ hours, or until the pork is golden brown. (If you prefer to use a meat thermometer, insert it into the pork loin before placing the loin in the casserole. Be sure the tip of the thermometer does not touch any bone. Roast the pork until the thermometer reaches a temperature of 175°.)

Cut away the strings and carve the pork into ½-inch-thick chops. Arrange the slices attractively in slightly overlapping layers on a large heated platter. Cover and set aside.

Strain the pan juices through a fine sieve set over a bowl, pressing down hard on the vegetables with the back of the spoon before discarding them. Skim as much fat as possible from the surface, then measure the juices. If there is more than 1½ cups, boil briskly over high heat until the juices are reduced to that amount; if there is less, add water. Bring the pan juices to a boil over moderate heat in a small saucepan. Give the cornstarch mixture a quick stir to recombine it and add it to the pan. Cook, stirring constantly, until the sauce clears and thickens slightly. Moisten the meat slices with a few spoonfuls of the sauce and serve the rest in a heated sauceboat.

Kasseler Rippenspeer is often served on a mound of either plain or pineapple sauerkraut *(page 62)*.

Falscher Wildschweinbraten

FRESH HAM, MOCK-BOAR STYLE

To serve 6 to 8

2 cups dry red wine
½ cup red wine vinegar
1 cup finely grated onions
15 whole juniper berries, crushed
  with a mortar and pestle or
  wrapped in a towel and crushed
  with a rolling pin
2 tablespoons grated fresh lemon
  peel
6 small bay leaves, coarsely crushed
2 teaspoons dried tarragon

1 teaspoon ground cloves
1 teaspoon ground allspice
1 teaspoon ground ginger
1 teaspoon freshly ground black
  pepper
A 5- to 6-pound fresh ham, rind
  removed and the ham trimmed of
  fat
1 tablespoon salt
2 tablespoons lard
2 cups water
3 tablespoons flour
3 tablespoons cold water

For the marinade pour the wine and vinegar into a mixing bowl and stir in the grated onions, juniper berries, grated lemon peel, bay leaves, tarragon, cloves, allspice, ginger and black pepper. Place the ham in a deep dish just large enough to hold it comfortably and pour the marinade over it. Cover with foil and marinate in the refrigerator for two days, turning it over once or twice a day.

Preheat the oven to 325°. Remove the ham from the marinade, and dry it thoroughly with paper towels, brushing off any bits of onion or herbs clinging to it. Rub the salt evenly into its surface. Strain the marinade into a bowl or saucepan, pressing down hard with a spoon on the solid ingredients to extract all their liquid before throwing them away.

In a heavy casserole or Dutch oven just large enough to hold the ham comfortably, melt the lard over high heat until a light haze forms above it. Add the ham and brown it well on all sides, turning the ham frequently and regulating the heat so the meat colors quickly and evenly without burning. Transfer the ham to a plate. Combine the strained marinade with 2 cups of water and pour the mixture into the casserole. Bring the liquid to a boil over high heat, meanwhile scraping in any brown bits clinging to the bottom and sides of the casserole.

Return the ham to the casserole, cover tightly, and bake in the middle of the oven for about 2 hours, basting it every 30 minutes or so with the cooking liquid. The ham is done when it can easily be pierced with the tip of a sharp knife. (You may use a meat thermometer, if you like, for more predictable results. After the ham is browned, insert the thermometer into the thickest part without letting the tip touch any bone. Roast until the thermometer reads 170° to 175°.) Transfer the ham to a heated platter and set it aside to rest for 10 to 15 minutes for easier carving.

Meanwhile, strain the cooking liquid into a small saucepan and skim off as much fat as possible from the surface. Measure the liquid, then boil it briskly to reduce it to 2 cups. Reduce the heat to low. Make a smooth paste of the flour and 3 tablespoons of cold water and, with a whisk or spoon, stir it gradually into the simmering liquid. Cook, stirring frequently, for about 10 minutes, or until the sauce thickens slightly. Taste for seasoning.

To serve, carve the ham into ¼-inch slices and arrange the slices attractively in overlapping layers on a large heated platter. Serve the sauce separately in a sauceboat.

Schinken in Burgunder
HAM BRAISED IN BURGUNDY

To serve 6 to 8

Half a precooked smoked ham, butt
   or shank end, about 5 to 6 pounds
2 cups water
2 cups red Burgundy or other dry
   red wine
1 medium-sized onion, peeled and
   thinly sliced
1 medium-sized tomato, peeled,
   seeded and coarsely chopped
1 whole clove, crushed with a mortar
   and pestle
1 small bay leaf
1 tablespoon butter, softened
1 tablespoon flour

Preheat the oven to 350°. With a small, sharp knife, separate the rind from the ham and place the rind in a 1- to 2-quart saucepan. Trim the ham of all but a ¼-inch layer of fat. Pour 2 cups of water over the rind, bring to a boil over high heat, then reduce the heat to low and simmer uncovered for 20 minutes. Strain the liquid through a sieve into a bowl and discard the rind.

Pour 1 cup of the rind stock into a shallow roasting pan just large enough to hold the ham comfortably. Add 1 cup of the wine, and the onion, tomato, clove and bay leaf. Place the ham, fat side up, in the pan and bake uncovered in the middle of the oven for about 1 hour. Baste the ham thoroughly every 20 minutes with the pan liquid. The ham is done when it can easily be pierced with a fork. Transfer the ham to a heated platter and let it rest for easier carving while you prepare the sauce.

Skim and discard all the fat from the pan liquid and stir in the remaining 1 cup of wine. Bring to a boil over high heat, meanwhile scraping in any brown bits clinging to the bottom or sides of the pan, and boil briskly for a minute or two. In a small bowl, make a paste of the butter and flour, and stir it bit by bit into the pan. Cook over low heat, stirring constantly, for 5 minutes, or until the sauce is smooth and slightly thickened. Strain it through a fine sieve into a small saucepan and taste for seasoning.

To serve, carve the ham into ¼-inch slices and arrange the slices attractively, in overlapping layers, on a large heated platter. Moisten the slices with a few spoonfuls of the Burgundy sauce, and serve the remaining sauce separately in a sauceboat.

Süss-saure Bratwurst

BRATWURST IN SWEET-SOUR SAUCE

To serve 4

8 bratwurst, separated
1 tablespoon dried black currants
4 whole allspice, pulverized with a
    mortar and pestle

2 cups cold water
1 tablespoon butter
2 tablespoons flour
2 teaspoons sugar
½ teaspoon salt
1 tablespoon fresh lemon juice

Place the bratwurst, currants and allspice in a 2- to 3-quart saucepan and pour in the water. Bring to a boil over high heat, reduce the heat to low and cover the pan. Simmer for 20 minutes, then set the sausages aside on a plate and cover with foil to keep them warm. Let the cooking liquid settle for a minute or two, and skim as much of the fat from the surface as possible.

In a heavy 8- to 10-inch skillet, melt the butter over moderate heat. Stir in the flour and cook, stirring constantly, for 3 to 4 minutes, or until the mixture colors lightly. Be careful it doesn't burn. Pour in 1 cup of the reserved cooking liquid including the currants. Stirring constantly with a whisk, bring the sauce to a boil. When it is thick and smooth, reduce the heat to low, stir in the sugar and salt and simmer for 3 to 4 minutes. Slice the sausages into ¼-inch rounds, add them to the sauce and simmer only long enough to heat them through. Just before serving, stir in the lemon juice and taste for seasoning. Transfer the entire contents of the skillet to a large, deep serving platter and serve at once.

Bratwurst mit saurer Sahnensosse

STEAMED BRATWURST IN SOUR-CREAM SAUCE

To serve 4

8 bratwurst sausages, separated
2 tablespoons butter

¼ cup cold water
1 tablespoon flour
½ teaspoon salt
1 cup sour cream

Drop the bratwurst into 2 quarts of boiling water, remove from the heat, and let the sausages soak for 5 minutes. Drain and pat the bratwurst dry with paper towels.

Melt the butter over moderate heat in a heavy 10- to 12-inch skillet, add the bratwurst and cook, turning them frequently with tongs until they are a golden brown on all sides. Add the ¼ cup of water to the skillet, reduce the heat, and simmer, uncovered, for 15 to 20 minutes, turning the bratwurst over after 10 minutes. Replenish the water with a few tablespoons of boiling water if the cooking water boils away. Transfer the sausages to a plate, and cover them with foil.

With a whisk, beat the flour and salt into the sour cream. Then, a few tablespoons at a time, stir the sour-cream mixture into the liquid remaining in the skillet. Cook over low heat, stirring constantly, for 5 to 8 minutes, until the sauce is smooth and slightly thickened. Do not let it boil. Slice the sausages into ¼-inch rounds, drop them into the skillet, baste with the sauce and simmer only long enough to heat the bratwurst through. Transfer the entire contents of the skillet to a large, deep platter and serve immediately.

Schweinerippchen mit Gewürzgurkensosse
SPARERIBS WITH PICKLE SAUCE

To serve 4

2 pounds spareribs, cut into serving pieces	together with a mortar and pestle or wrapped in a towel and crushed with a rolling pin
1 teaspoon salt	1 small bay leaf
Freshly ground black pepper	1 tablespoon flour
2 tablespoons lard	2 tablespoons tomato purée
1 cup finely chopped onions	1 cup finely diced dill pickle
2 whole allspice and 1 clove, crushed	2 cups water

Sprinkle the spareribs on both sides with the salt and a few grindings of black pepper. In a heavy 12-inch skillet melt the lard over high heat until a light haze forms above it. Add the spareribs and brown them thoroughly on both sides regulating the heat so that they color evenly without burning. Remove them to a plate. To the fat remaining in the skillet, add the onions, the crushed allspice and clove and the bay leaf, then stir in the flour and tomato purée. Mix vigorously with a wooden spoon until the ingredients are thoroughly combined. Add the pickle and then pour in the 2 cups of water. Bring to a boil, meanwhile stirring with a whisk until the sauce thickens lightly. Reduce the heat to low and return the browned spareribs to the skillet. Baste them well with the sauce and cover the pan. Basting occasionally, simmer for an hour until the ribs are tender and can easily be pierced with the tip of a small, sharp knife. Remove the bay leaf. To serve, arrange the spareribs on a large, heated platter and pour the sauce over them.

Pichelsteiner Fleisch

MIXED MEAT AND VEGETABLE CASSEROLE

To serve 6

2 to 4 tablespoons lard
½ pound boneless shoulder of lamb,
    cut into 1-inch cubes
½ pound boneless beef chuck, cut
    into 1-inch cubes
½ pound boneless veal, cut into
    1-inch cubes
½ pound boneless pork, cut into
    1-inch cubes
2 cups cold water
2 cups scraped carrots, cut into
    1-inch lengths
1½ cups cored savoy or green
    cabbage, cut into 1½-by-1-inch
    pieces
1 cup fresh green beans, cut into
    1½-inch lengths
1 cup peeled celery root (celeriac),

cut into ½-inch dice
1 cup scraped parsnips, cut into
    1-inch lengths
1 cup leeks, sliced into 1-inch
    lengths (including 1 inch of the
    green part)
½ cup kohlrabi, if available, cut
    into ¼-inch slices
½ cup freshly shelled green peas,
    or substitute ½ cup thoroughly
    defrosted frozen green peas
½ cup coarsely chopped onions
Salt
Freshly ground black pepper
¼ pound beef marrow, coarsely
    diced
3 medium-sized boiling potatoes
    (about 1 pound), peeled and cut
    into ½-inch cubes

In a heavy 10- to 12-inch skillet heat 2 tablespoons of the lard over high heat until a light haze forms above it. Add the cubed lamb, beef, veal and pork (in any order you like) a few pieces at a time, and brown them well on all sides, regulating the heat so the cubes brown quickly and evenly without burning. Replenish the lard in the pan as needed, and transfer the browned meats to a bowl as you proceed.

When all the meat is browned, pour the 2 cups of water into the skillet and bring to a boil, meanwhile scraping in any brown particles clinging to the bottom and sides of the pan. Boil briskly for a few seconds, then set the skillet aside off the heat.

In a large mixing bowl combine the carrots, cabbage, green beans, celery root, parsnips, leeks, kohlrabi, peas, onions, ½ teaspoon of salt and a few grindings of black pepper. Toss the vegetables about with a spoon to mix them thoroughly.

Spread the marrow in the bottom of a heavy 6-quart casserole, and arrange about a third of the meat cubes over it. Sprinkle the meat with a little salt and freshly ground pepper and spread it with a third of the mixed vegetables. Repeat the layers in thirds similarly. Scatter the diced potatoes over the final layer of vegetables, sprinkle lightly with salt and pepper, and pour in the reserved liquid.

Bring to a boil over high heat, then reduce the heat to its lowest point and cover the casserole tightly. Simmer, without stirring at any point, for 1½ hours. Serve directly from the casserole.

NOTE: Traditionally, this dish is made from whatever vegetables are in season, but in modern Germany frozen vegetables are often substituted for the fresh ones. Celery may replace celery root, and additional onions may replace the leeks. Be sure to use 8 or 9 cups of vegetables, whichever they are.

Labskaus

CORNED BEEF HASH WITH SALT HERRING

To serve 4 to 6

¼ pound filleted salt herring
9 medium-sized boiling potatoes
    (about 3 pounds), unpeeled
6 tablespoons lard

1½ pounds cooked brisket of corned
    beef, trimmed of fat and cut into
    ⅛-inch dice
2½ cups finely chopped onions
Freshly ground black pepper
Ground nutmeg

Place the herring fillets in a glass or enameled bowl and pour in enough water to cover them by about 1 inch. Refrigerate and soak for at least 12 hours, changing the water once or twice. Drain and rinse the fillets under cold running water, then pat them dry with paper towels. Remove any skin or bones and, with a large knife, chop the herring as finely as possible.

Drop the potatoes into a large pot of lightly salted boiling water, and boil them briskly, uncovered, until they show no resistance when pierced with the tip of a small, sharp knife. Drain and peel them, then force them through a ricer or food mill into a large bowl.

In a heavy 12-inch skillet, melt the 6 tablespoons of lard over moderate heat until a light haze forms above it. Add the herring, corned beef and onions, lower the heat and cook, stirring frequently, for 20 minutes, watching carefully for any sign of burning, and regulating the heat accordingly. Stir in the potatoes, pepper and nutmeg and simmer only long enough to heat the mixture through. If the hash seems too dry and begins to stick to the pan, moisten it with a little water. Taste for seasoning, and mound the hash attractively on a large heated platter. *Labskaus* may be served with a poached egg on each portion and accompanied by pickled beets *(page 75)*.

Gebratene Kalbsleber auf Berliner Art
CALF'S LIVER WITH APPLES AND ONION RINGS

To serve 3 or 4

8 tablespoons butter
2 medium-sized onions, cut into ⅛-
inch slices and separated into rings
Salt
Freshly ground black pepper

5 medium-sized cooking apples
(about 1½ pounds), peeled, cored
and sliced crosswise into ¼-inch
rings
1 pound calf's liver, cut into ¼-
inch slices
Flour

Preheat the oven to 250°. In a heavy 10- to 12-inch skillet, melt 2 table-spoons of the butter over moderate heat. When the foam subsides, add the onion rings, a little salt and a few grindings of pepper. Stirring occasionally, cook the onion rings for about 10 minutes, or until they are light brown. With a slotted spoon, transfer them to a heatproof plate, cover them loosely with aluminum foil and place them in the preheated oven. Add 2 tablespoons of butter to the skillet and drop in half of the apple rings. Cook them until they are golden on both sides, add them to the plate with the onion rings and cook the remaining apple slices similarly in another 2 tablespoons of but-ter. Keep the apples and onions warm in the oven while you cook the liver.

Season the liver slices with salt and a few grindings of pepper. Dip the slices in flour, then vigorously shake off any excess. Add the remaining 2 ta-blespoons of butter to the skillet and melt the butter over moderate heat. When the foam subsides add the liver and cook it for 2 minutes on each side, or until the slices are light brown, turning them with kitchen tongs. Do not overcook. Remove the liver to a heated platter and scatter the apple and onion rings over it and serve at once.

Gänsebraten mit Äpfeln, Rosinen und Nüssen
ROAST GOOSE WITH APPLE, RAISIN AND NUT STUFFING

To serve 6 to 8

An 8- to 10-pound young goose
and its giblets
1 cup seedless raisins
3 tablespoons butter
1 cup finely chopped onions
4 cups soft white bread crumbs,
made from fresh, homemade-type
white bread pulverized in a blender
or pulled apart and shredded with
a fork

3 medium-sized cooking apples,
peeled, cored and coarsely
chopped
½ cup coarsely chopped blanched
hazelnuts or almonds
¼ cup finely chopped parsley
1 teaspoon dried marjoram
1 teaspoon salt
Freshly ground black pepper

In a small saucepan, combine the goose gizzard and heart with enough water to cover them completely. Bring to a boil over high heat, reduce the heat to low and simmer uncovered for 40 minutes, or until they show no resistance when pierced with the tip of a small, sharp knife. Meanwhile, place the raisins in a bowl and pour 2 cups of boiling water over them. Let them soak for 20 minutes, or until plump. Drain the gizzard and heart, chop them fine and place them in a large mixing bowl. Add the drained raisins.

Preheat the oven to 325°. In a heavy 8- to 10-inch skillet, melt the butter over moderate heat. When the foam has almost subsided, add the onions and cook, stirring frequently, for 5 minutes, or until they are soft and transparent but not brown. Chop the goose liver into fine dice, add it to the onions, and cook, stirring constantly, for 2 or 3 minutes, or until the liver is light brown. With a rubber spatula, scrape the entire contents of the skillet into the mixing bowl. Add the bread crumbs, apples, chopped nuts, parsley, marjoram, salt and a few grindings of pepper, and toss the mixture together with a spoon until the ingredients are well combined. Taste for seasoning.

Wash the goose under cold, running water and pat it thoroughly dry inside and out with paper towels. Lightly salt and pepper the cavity and fill it loosely with the stuffing. Close the opening by lacing it with skewers or sewing it with a large needle and heavy white thread. Fasten the neck skin to the back of the goose with a skewer and truss the bird securely. For a crisper skin, prick the surface around the thighs, the back, and the lower part of the breast with the tip of a small, sharp knife.

Place the goose breast side up on a rack set in a large, shallow roasting pan, and roast in the middle of the oven for 3 to 3½ hours, or about 20 minutes to the pound. As the fat accumulates in the pan, draw it off with a bulb baster or large kitchen spoon and, if you like, save it for another use. Basting the goose is unnecessary. To test for doneness, pierce the thigh of the bird with the tip of a small, sharp knife. The juice that runs out should be pale yellow; if it is tinged with pink, roast the goose another 5 to 10 minutes. Let the goose rest in the turned-off oven with the door ajar for about 15 minutes for easier carving.

Transfer the goose to a large, heated platter and remove the string and skewers. Traditionally, roast goose is served with red cabbage (page 63).

Berliner Hühnerfrikassee

BERLIN-STYLE CHICKEN FRICASSEE

To serve 8

TONGUE

A 1-pound fresh veal tongue	A bouquet made of 2 celery tops
1 medium-sized onion, peeled and	and 2 parsley sprigs, tied together
quartered	½ teaspoon salt

TONGUE: In a large saucepan, combine the tongue, quartered onion, bouquet and salt. Pour in enough cold water to cover the tongue by at least 2 inches, and bring to a boil over high heat. Reduce the heat to low, partially cover the pan and simmer for about 2 hours, or until the meat shows no resistance when pierced with the tip of a sharp knife. Add boiling water to the pan if needed; the tongue should be covered with water throughout the cooking period. Remove the tongue from the stock and while it is still hot, skin it with a small, sharp knife, cutting away the fat, bones and gristle at its base. Cut the tongue into ½-inch slices, then into ½-inch dice and set aside in a bowl. Discard the cooking liquid and vegetables.

SWEETBREADS

1 pair veal sweetbreads (about ¾	Vinegar
pound)	1 teaspoon fresh lemon juice
	2 teaspoons salt

SWEETBREADS: Soak the sweetbreads in enough cold water to cover them for 2 hours, changing the water ever 30 minutes or so. Then soak them for another hour in acidulated cold water, using 1 tablespoon of vinegar for each quart of water. Gently pull off as much of the outside membrane as possible without tearing the sweetbreads. Cut the two lobes of the pair of sweetbreads from the tube between them with a small, sharp knife; discard the tube. Place the sweetbreads in an enameled saucepan with enough water to cover them by 2 inches, add the lemon juice and salt and bring to a boil. Reduce the heat to its lowest point and simmer uncovered for 15 to 20 minutes, or until the sweetbreads are tender when pierced with the tip of a fork. Drain and dry with paper towels. Then cut them into ½-inch dice and set them aside in a bowl.

CHICKEN

A 4-pound fowl or roasting chicken	2 medium-sized onions, peeled and
2 carrots, scraped and coarsely	coarsely chopped
chopped	4 parsley sprigs
2 leeks, including 2 inches of green,	1 tablespoon salt
coarsely chopped	10 cups water

CHICKEN: In a 6-quart soup pot, combine the chicken, chopped carrots, leeks, chopped onions, parsley and 1 tablespoon salt. Add 10 cups of cold water, then bring to a boil over high heat, reduce the heat to low, partially cover the pot and simmer for 2½ to 3 hours if you are using a fowl, or for 1½ to 2 hours if you are using a roasting chicken. When the chicken is tender but not falling apart, take it from the pot. When it is cool enough to handle remove its skin with a small, sharp knife, and cut the meat away from the bones. Return the skin and bones to the stock, cut the chicken meat into ½-inch dice and set aside in a bowl covered with plastic wrap. Bring the stock remaining in the pot to a boil, again, reduce the heat and simmer for 30 minutes longer. Then strain it through a fine sieve set over a mixing bowl and set it aside.

ASPARAGUS
1 pound fresh asparagus   2 teaspoons salt

ASPARAGUS: With a small, sharp knife, cut off the butt ends of the asparagus spears and peel the tough skin from the lower end of each spear. Wash the spears under cold running water and divide them into 2 equal bunches. Tie each bunch together with loops of string at each end. In an enameled or stainless-steel pot large enough to hold the asparagus horizontally, bring 4 quarts of water and 2 teaspoons of salt to a bubbling boil. Drop in the asparagus, bring the water to a boil, reduce the heat to moderate and cook uncovered for 8 to 10 minutes, or until the butt ends are tender but still slightly resistant when pierced with the tip of a sharp knife. With two kitchen forks, lift the bundles out of the water by their strings and drain them on paper towels. Cut the stalks into 1-inch lengths and set aside.

SHRIMP   (about 26 to 30 per pound)
1 pound raw shrimp in their shells   1 teaspoon salt

SHRIMP: Shell the shrimp, and with a small, sharp knife, make a shallow incision down the back of each shrimp and lift out the black or white intestinal vein. Wash the shrimp under cold running water. Bring 2 quarts of water and 1 teaspoon salt to a boil in a 3- to 4-quart saucepan. Drop in the shrimp, reduce the heat to moderate and boil uncovered for 3 to 4 minutes, or until the shrimp turn pink and are firm. Do not overcook. Drain and set them aside.

MUSHROOMS
½ pound small fresh mushrooms,   1 teaspoon salt
   trimmed and sliced thinly   1 teaspoon fresh lemon juice

MUSHROOMS: Wipe the mushrooms with a damp paper towel and cut away the tough ends of the mushroom stems. Bring 3 cups of water, 1 tea-

Continued on next page   41

spoon salt and 1 teaspoon of lemon juice to a boil in a 2- to 3-quart enameled or stainless-steel saucepan and drop in the mushrooms. Reduce the heat to low, cover and simmer for about 3 minutes. Drain thoroughly, let the mushrooms cool, and chop them into fine dice. Set aside.

SAUCE

6 tablespoons butter	3 egg yolks
6 tablespoons flour	3 tablespoons fresh lemon juice

SAUCE: Skim the fat from the surface of the reserved chicken stock. In a 2-quart enameled or stainless-steel saucepan, melt 6 tablespoons of butter over moderate heat. When the foam subsides, stir in the flour. Pour in 6 cups of the stock and, beating vigorously with a whisk, bring the sauce to a boil. When it is quite thick and smooth, reduce the heat to low and simmer slowly for 5 minutes. Break up the egg yolks with a fork, then stir in ¼ cup of the simmering sauce. Whisk the egg-yolk mixture into the pan and bring the sauce to a boil, over moderate heat, stirring constantly. Boil for 30 seconds, remove from the heat and stir in the 3 tablespoons of lemon juice. Taste for seasoning.

TO ASSEMBLE: In a large heavy casserole combine the sauce with the reserved tongue, sweetbreads, chicken, shrimp and mushrooms but do not include any juices which may have accumulated around them. Add the asparagus, and stir together gently but thoroughly with a large spoon. Taste for seasoning. Simmer over moderate heat, stirring occasionally, until the mixture is heated through. Serve directly from the casserole.

NOTE: Morel mushrooms are often added to the fricassee and you may include ½ cup of them if you like. Dried morels must be soaked in 4 or 5 changes of cold water to remove all sand. Cover the morels with water, let them soak for about 30 minutes, then rinse them under running water squeezing out as much grit as possible. Repeat until the morels are completely clean. Simmer them in lightly salted boiling water to cover for 10 minutes, or until tender, drain thoroughly and cut them into quarters. Canned morels only need to be drained well, rinsed under cold running water, and cut into quarters. Whichever kind you are using, add them to the sauce along with the fresh mushrooms.

Ente mit Äpfeln und Brot Füllung
ROAST DUCK WITH APPLE AND BREAD STUFFING

To serve 4

A 4½- to 5-pound duck
Salt
Freshly ground black pepper
¾ pound lean ground beef,
    preferably chuck

¾ pound lean ground pork
1 egg, lightly beaten
½ cup dried bread crumbs
½ teaspoon dried marjoram
2 medium-sized cooking apples,
    peeled, cored and cut into
    ½-inch cubes

Preheat the oven to 425°. Wash the duck under cold running water and pat dry inside and out with paper towels. Rub the inside of the duck liberally with salt and pepper. For crisper skin, prick the surface around the thighs, the back, and the lower part of the breast with the tip of a sharp knife.

In a large bowl, combine the beef, pork, egg, crumbs, marjoram, 1 teaspoon of salt and a few grindings of pepper. Knead vigorously with both hands until the ingredients are well blended and the mixture is smooth. Then stir in the apples and spoon the stuffing loosely into the cavity. Close the opening by lacing it with skewers or sewing it with heavy thread. Fasten the neck skin to the back of the duck with a skewer and truss the bird securely.

Roast the duck, breast side up on a rack set in a large shallow pan, for 20 minutes, until it browns lightly. Pour off the fat from the roasting pan or draw it off with a bulb baster. Then reduce the heat to 350°, and roast for about 1 hour longer, removing the accumulated fat from the pan occasionally with a bulb baster. To test for doneness, pierce the thigh of the bird with the tip of a small, sharp knife. The juice should spurt out a clear yellow; if it is slightly pink, roast the bird for another 5 to 10 minutes. Transfer the duck to a heated platter and let it rest for 10 minutes before carving. Traditionally the duck is accompanied by red cabbage *(page 63)* and dumplings.

Game

Hasenpfeffer

BRAISED RABBIT IN SPICED RED WINE SAUCE

To serve 6

½ pound lean bacon, finely chopped
A 5- to 6-pound fresh rabbit or
   defrosted frozen mature rabbit, cut
   in serving pieces, or substitute two
   2½- to 3-pound fresh or defrosted
   frozen rabbits, cut in serving
   pieces
½ teaspoon salt
½ teaspoon freshly ground black
   pepper
½ cup flour

½ cup finely chopped shallots, or
   substitute ½ cup finely chopped
   onions
½ teaspoon finely chopped garlic
1 cup dry red wine
1 cup chicken stock, fresh or canned
2 tablespoons brandy
1 teaspoon currant jelly
1 small bay leaf
⅛ teaspoon dried rosemary
⅛ teaspoon dried thyme
2 teaspoons fresh lemon juice

In a heavy 5-quart flameproof casserole, cook the bacon over moderate heat, stirring and turning it frequently, until it is crisp. Spread the bacon out on a double thickness of paper towels to drain and set the casserole with the bacon fat aside.

Wash the rabbit quickly under cold running water and pat it thoroughly dry with paper towels. Sprinkle the pieces with salt and pepper, then dip them in flour and shake off any excess. Heat the bacon fat in the casserole over high heat until it splutters. Add the rabbit, a few pieces at a time, and brown them on all sides, regulating the heat so that they color quickly and evenly without burning. As they are done, transfer the rabbit pieces to a plate. Pour off all but 2 tablespoons of fat from the casserole and in it cook the shallots and garlic, stirring frequently, for 4 or 5 minutes, or until the shallots are soft and transparent but not brown. Pour in the wine and stock, and bring to a boil over high heat, meanwhile scraping in any brown bits clinging to the bottom and sides of the pan. Stir in the brandy, currant jelly, bay leaf, rosemary and thyme, and return the rabbit and any juices collected around it to the casserole. Add the drained bacon, cover the casserole tightly, and simmer over low heat for 1½ hours, or until the rabbit is tender but not falling apart. (If you are substituting small rabbits, they may cook much faster. Test them for doneness after about 1 hour of cooking.) Pick out the bay leaf, stir in the lemon juice and taste for seasoning. The sauce should be quite peppery; add more pepper, if necessary, to taste.

Serve the rabbit directly from the casserole, or arrange the pieces attractively on a deep heated platter and pour the sauce over them.

NOTE: Traditionally, the sauce in which the rabbit is simmered is thickened, just before serving, with the rabbit's blood. If you hunt and dress your own rabbit, save its blood. Stir into it 1 or 2 tablespoons of vinegar to prevent it from clotting and refrigerate until ready to use. Stir the blood into the sauce after the rabbit is cooked, then simmer gently, stirring all the while, for 4 or 5 minutes, or until the sauce thickens slightly. Be careful not to let the sauce boil. Add the lemon juice, taste for seasoning and serve.

Rehschnitzel mit Pilzen
VENISON CUTLETS WITH MUSHROOMS

To serve 6

10 whole juniper berries	preferably from the leg, cut ½ inch thick and pounded slightly
5 whole black peppercorns	½ cup plus 1 tablespoon flour
1 small bay leaf, crumbled	4 tablespoons butter
½ teaspoon salt	1 cup thinly sliced fresh mushrooms
6 six-ounce venison cutlets,	¼ cup light cream

With a mortar and pestle, pulverize the juniper berries, peppercorns, crumbled bay leaf and salt together. Then firmly press the mixture with your fingertips into both sides of the venison cutlets. Dip the cutlets in ½ cup of the flour and shake off any excess. In a heavy 12-inch skillet, melt the butter over moderate heat. When the foam subsides, add the cutlets (in two batches if they crowd the pan), and cook them for 2 or 3 minutes on each side, regulating the heat so that they color evenly without burning. Don't overcook; when done, the cutlets should be slightly pink inside. Place the cutlets side by side on a heated platter and cover with foil to keep them warm while you prepare the sauce.

Add the sliced mushrooms to the fat remaining in the skillet and cook them over moderate heat, stirring frequently, for 3 or 4 minutes. Then stir in 1 tablespoon of flour and cook, stirring constantly, for a minute or two. Add the cream and cook, stirring until the sauce thickens slightly. Taste for seasoning. Pour the sauce over the cutlets and serve.

NOTE: In Germany, the venison cutlets are sautéed in butter alone. To avoid the danger of burning the butter, you may prefer to use 3 tablespoons of butter combined with 1 tablespoon of vegetable oil.

How to Lard a Saddle of Venison

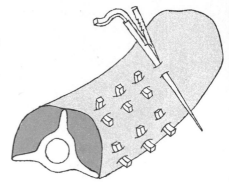

Larding a saddle of venison takes only minutes—and keeps the roast moist. If you have a larding needle with a clip, insert one lardon into it at a time and, as shown at right, make 1-inch larding stitches through the meat. Space the stitches as evenly as you can, about an inch apart in two rows across both sides of the saddle. Snip off the ends of the lardons as you go. If you do not have a needle, cut the lardons into 2½-inch lengths, make holes for them with the tip of a skewer, an ice pick or a small, sharp knife, and poke them into place.

Carving the Venison

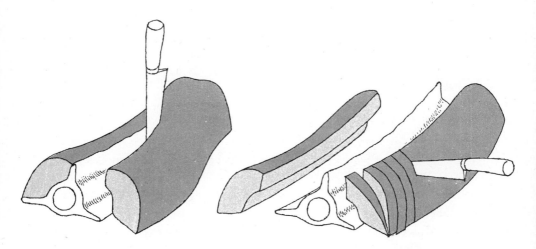

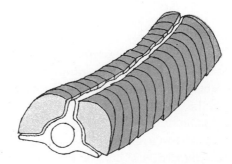

Stand the saddle on its rib side, then cut each loin entirely away from the backbone and rib bones (above). Carve the loins crosswise into ¼-inch slices, cutting at a slight diagonal so the first slice at each end is a tapered wedge (above, right). Reassemble the saddle (right) on a platter, and it is ready to serve.

Rehrücken mit Rotweinsosse
ROAST SADDLE OF VENISON WITH RED WINE SAUCE

To serve 6 to 8

3 cups dry red wine

3 cups cold water

5 whole juniper berries, 2 whole cloves and 8 whole black peppercorns, bruised with a mortar and pestle or wrapped in a towel and bruised with a rolling pin

1 large bay leaf

1 tablespoon salt

A 5-pound saddle of venison

4 ounces slab bacon, sliced ⅛ inch thick and cut into lardons ⅛ inch wide and about 8 to 10 inches long

4 tablespoons lard

1 cup thinly sliced scraped carrots

½ cup finely chopped onions

¼ cup thinly sliced leeks, white part only

1½ cups thinly sliced celery, including some of the leaves

3 tablespoons flour

½ cup sour cream

1 teaspoon fresh lemon juice

4 poached fresh pears or 8 canned pear halves, thoroughly drained (optional)

½ cup lingonberry (*Preiselbeeren*) preserves (optional)

In a heavy 3- to 4-quart stainless-steel or enameled saucepan, bring the wine, water, juniper berries, cloves, peppercorns, bay leaf and the salt to a boil over high heat. Remove the pan from the heat and let the marinade cool to room temperature.

Place the venison in an enameled or stainless-steel roasting pan just large enough to hold it comfortably and pour in the marinade. Turn the meat to moisten it thoroughly on all sides. Marinate at room temperature for at least 6 hours, turning the venison once or twice. Or cover it tightly with foil or plastic wrap and marinate in the refrigerator for as long as 3 days, turning the venison over at least once each day. Because marinades are tenderizers, the older the animal, the longer it should marinate.

Remove the venison from the marinade and set the marinade aside in a bowl. Pat the meat completely dry with paper towels and lard it in the following fashion: Insert the tip of a bacon lardon into the clip of a larding needle. Force it through the roast by pushing the point of the needle into the surface of the meat at an angle toward the backbone. Pull the needle through and trim the ends of the lardon so that ¼ inch protrudes from each end of the stitch. Space the lardons about an inch apart in 2 horizontal rows along both sides of the saddle.

If you do not have a larding needle, cut the lardons into short strips about 2½ inches long. Make small stitchlike holes through the surface of the meat with a skewer, ice pick or small knife, and use its tip to push the short lardons through the holes.

Preheat the oven to 350°. Dry the roasting pan and in it melt the lard over high heat until it splutters. Add the saddle and brown it on all sides, reg-

Continued on next page 47

ulating the heat so that the meat colors evenly without burning.

Transfer the saddle to a platter, and add the carrots, onions, leeks and celery to the fat remaining in the pan. Cook over moderate heat, stirring frequently, for 4 or 5 minutes, or until the vegetables are soft and lightly colored. Sprinkle 3 tablespoons of flour over the vegetables and cook over low heat, stirring constantly, for 2 or 3 minutes to brown the flour slightly. Watch carefully for any sign of burning.

Now place the venison on top of the vegetables and pour in enough of the marinade to come about 2 inches up the side of the saddle. (Reserve the remaining marinade.) Roast the venison, uncovered, in the middle of the oven for 1½ hours, or until the meat is tender (ideally it should be slightly pink), basting it occasionally with the pan juices, and adding more marinade to the pan if the liquid cooks away. Transfer the venison to a large heated platter and let it rest for 10 minutes or so for easier carving.

Strain the liquid in the roasting pan through a fine sieve into an 8-inch skillet, pressing down hard on the vegetables with the back of a spoon before discarding them. Skim thoroughly of all surface fat. There should be about 2 cups of liquid. If more, boil it rapidly over high heat until reduced to the required amount; if less, add as much of the reserved marinade as necessary. Bring to a boil over high heat. Reduce the heat to low and add the sour cream, whisking constantly. Simmer the sauce for 5 minutes, whisking occasionally, then stir in the lemon juice. Taste for seasoning.

To carve the saddle, separate each loin from the bones by holding the carving knife against the ridge on either side of the backbone and cutting down through the meat along the contours of the bones. Cut the loins crosswise into ¼-inch slices as shown in the diagrams below, carving at a slight angle so that the first slice from each loin is tapered. Reassemble the saddle on the platter and garnish it, if you like, with pear halves filled with lingonberry (*Preiselbeeren*) preserves.

Traditionally, the roast saddle of venison is also accompanied by a variety of such vegetables as green beans, carrots, mushrooms and red cabbage.

NOTE: To poach fresh pears, peel them, cut them in half lengthwise and scoop out the cores with a teaspoon. In a 10- to 12-inch enameled or stainless-steel skillet, combine 4 cups of water, 2 tablespoons of sugar and 1 teaspoon of fresh lemon juice. Bring to a boil, add the pears, reduce the heat to low and simmer uncovered for 5 to 15 minutes, or until the pears show almost no resistance when pierced with a fork. Baste the pears occasionally if they are not completely covered by the liquid. Drain, cool to room temperature and refrigerate until ready to serve.

If a saddle of venison is not available, a 4- to 5-pound boned and rolled venison leg or shoulder roast may be substituted. In that case leave the lardons in long strips and insert them completely through the meat from one end of the roast to the other.

Piquante Rehfiletschnitten

VENISON TENDERLOIN IN SPICED BRANDY SAUCE

To serve 4

½ cup dry red wine
½ cup water
1 medium-sized onion, peeled and
cut into ⅛-inch slices
2 tablespoons finely chopped
shallots, or substitute 2
tablespoons finely chopped
scallions
A 2-inch piece of cinnamon stick
1 small bay leaf

1 whole clove
3 parsley sprigs
⅛ teaspoon thyme
½ teaspoon salt
Freshly ground black pepper
2 pounds venison tenderloin, cut
into ¼-inch-thick slices
3 tablespoons butter
2 tablespoons flour
½ cup chicken stock
2 tablespoons brandy

In a small mixing bowl, combine the red wine, water, sliced onion, shallots, cinnamon, bay leaf, clove, parsley, thyme, salt and a few grindings of pepper. Arrange the venison slices in one layer in a shallow baking dish and pour the marinade over them, turning the steaks to moisten them thoroughly. Marinate at room temperature for at least 2 hours, turning the steaks once or twice.

Preheat the oven to 300°. Remove the steaks from the marinade and pat them thoroughly dry. Set the marinade aside. In a heavy 10- to 12-inch skillet, melt the butter over moderate heat. When the foam subsides, add the venison steaks and brown them for 2 or 3 minutes on each side, regulating the heat so they color quickly and evenly and without burning. Transfer the steaks to a shallow casserole or baking dish just large enough to hold them comfortably in one layer, and set them aside.

Strain the marinade through a fine sieve set over a bowl, pressing down hard on the vegetables with the back of a spoon before discarding them. Add the flour to the fat remaining in the skillet, and cook over moderate heat, stirring constantly, until the flour browns lightly. Gradually pour in the strained marinade, chicken stock and brandy. Stirring constantly with a whisk, bring it to a boil, continuing to stir until the sauce is smooth and slightly thickened. Taste for seasoning. Pour the sauce over the venison steaks and bake in the middle of the oven for 10 minutes, basting them occasionally with the pan juices. Serve at once, directly from the casserole, or on a large heated platter.

NOTE: In Germany the venison is browned in butter as described above. Because butter alone burns easily, you may prefer to use 2 tablespoons of butter combined with 1 tablespoon of vegetable oil.

Rebhühner mit Weintrauben
ROAST PARTRIDGES WITH GRAPES

To serve 4

10 slices lean bacon
4 partridge hearts, gizzards and livers
4 one-pound oven-ready young
   partridges
Salt
Freshly ground black pepper
8 whole juniper berries, coarsely
   crushed with a mortar and pestle

2 cups seeded green or red grapes,
   or 2 cups green seedless grapes
8 canned grape leaves, or 8 washed
   fresh grape leaves
½ cup dry white or red wine
¾ cup chicken stock, fresh or
   canned
½ cup sour cream
3 or 4 small bunches of green or
   red grapes (optional)

Preheat the oven to 400°. Cook 2 of the bacon slices over low heat in a small skillet only until they are somewhat translucent and soft but not brown. Drain them on a double thickness of paper towels and then cut each strip into 6 equal pieces. Wash the hearts, gizzards and livers of the birds and pat them dry with paper towels. Then wrap them individually in small pieces of the cooked bacon, keeping the giblets for each bird aside separately.

Wash the partridges quickly under running water and dry them thoroughly inside and out with paper towels. Sprinkle the cavities of the birds with salt and a few grindings of pepper, then stuff each bird with its wrapped giblets together with 2 of the juniper berries and ½ cup of the grapes. Neatly truss the partridges with white kitchen string. Drape 2 uncooked slices of bacon across the breast and thighs of each bird, pressing the bacon snugly against the bird to keep it in place. Drape 2 grape leaves over each partridge.

Place the birds on their backs on a rack in a large, shallow roasting pan and roast them in the middle of the oven for 20 minutes, basting them every 10 minutes with 2 tablespoons of the wine. Reduce the heat to 350°, and carefully remove and discard the grape leaves and bacon from the birds. Continue roasting for 15 to 20 minutes, basting every 5 minutes or so with the remaining wine and then with the juices as they collect in the pan. The birds are done when they are a golden brown and the drumsticks feel tender to the touch. Remove the string, transfer the partridges to a heated platter and cover loosely with foil to keep them warm while you make the sauce.

Pour the pan juices through a fine sieve set over a mixing bowl. Measure the strained liquid, add enough chicken stock to make 1¼ cups and pour it into a small saucepan. Bring to a boil over high heat, reduce the heat to low and beat in the sour cream, a few tablespoonfuls at a time. Cook for a moment or two to heat the cream through. Do not let it boil. Taste and season with as much salt and pepper as you think it needs. Then spoon the sauce over the partridges and serve at once. Traditionally, the birds are accompanied by *Weinkraut (page 62)* and mashed potatoes. If you like, you may garnish the partridges with bunches of grapes or line the platter with additional grape leaves, arrange the birds on the leaves and garnish them with grapes. Then serve the sauce separately in a sauceboat.

Wildgeflügel mit Burgunder
GAME BIRDS IN BURGUNDY

To serve 4

4 one-pound, oven-ready young partridge, baby pheasant, quail, woodcock or grouse
Salt
Freshly ground black pepper
1 cup flour
7 tablespoons butter
¼ cup finely chopped shallots
2 cups thinly sliced mushrooms

(about ½ pound)
2 tablespoons finely chopped cooked ham
2 cups Burgundy or other dry red wine
2 tablespoons brandy
⅛ teaspoon dried thyme
⅛ teaspoon dried tarragon
½ small bay leaf
Pinch of ground nutmeg
2 tablespoons finely chopped parsley

Wash the birds quickly under running water and dry them inside and out with paper towels. Season the birds generously with salt and pepper, roll them in flour, then vigorously shake off the excess. In a heavy 10- to 12-inch skillet, melt 3 tablespoons of the butter over moderate heat. When the foam subsides, brown the birds, turning them frequently, until they are a light golden color on all sides. Remove the birds from the skillet and set aside. Melt 2 more tablespoons of butter in the skillet. Add 3 tablespoons of shallots and cook them over moderate heat, stirring frequently, for 4 or 5 minutes, then drop in the mushroom slices and chopped ham. Cook, stirring occasionally, for 3 to 4 minutes, until the mushrooms are lightly browned. With a rubber spatula, transfer the mixture to a bowl and set aside.

Melt the remaining 2 tablespoons of butter in the skillet and in it cook the remaining 1 tablespoon of shallots for 2 or 3 minutes, until they are soft and lightly colored. Add the wine and brandy, and bring to a boil over high heat, meanwhile scraping in any brown bits clinging to the bottom and sides of the pan. Add the thyme, tarragon, bay leaf, nutmeg, ½ teaspoon of salt and a few grindings of black pepper, stir, and then return the birds to the skillet. Baste the birds thoroughly, reduce the heat to low, cover the skillet and simmer for 20 to 30 minutes, or until the birds are tender. Test by pressing a drumstick with your finger; it should show no resistance when the bird is fully cooked. Transfer the birds to a heated platter and cover them with foil; let them rest while you prepare the sauce.

Bring the juices remaining in the skillet to a boil, and boil briskly until the liquid is reduced to about 1 cup. Remove the bay leaf, stir in the mushroom-ham mixture and simmer for a minute or two. Taste for seasoning, and stir in the parsley. Pour the sauce into a sauceboat and serve with the birds.

Fasan in Rotwein

PHEASANT IN RED WINE

To serve 4 to 6

A 3½- to 4-pound oven-ready
   pheasant
6 tablespoons butter, softened
Salt
Freshly ground black pepper
½ cup finely chopped onions

1 cup dry red wine
½ cup cold water or ½ cup chicken
   stock, fresh or canned
½ small bay leaf
2 slices lean bacon
1 cup thinly sliced fresh mushrooms
1 tablespoon flour
⅓ cup heavy cream

Wash the pheasant quickly under cold running water and pat it thoroughly dry inside and out with paper towels. Then rub the cavity of the bird with 1 tablespoon of the soft butter and sprinkle it liberally with salt and a few grindings of pepper. Truss the bird securely with white kitchen cord.

In a heavy 5-quart casserole or Dutch oven, heat 3 tablespoons of the butter over moderate heat, add the pheasant and brown it well on all sides, turning it frequently and regulating the heat so that the bird browns quickly without burning. Transfer the pheasant to a plate. Add the chopped onions to the casserole and cook over moderate heat for 5 to 8 minutes, stirring occasionally, until the onions are soft and light brown. Then pour in the wine and bring it to a boil, meanwhile scraping into it any brown bits clinging to the bottom and sides of the casserole. Stir in the water or stock, bay leaf, ½ teaspoon of salt and a few grindings of black pepper.

Return the pheasant and any juices that have accumulated around it to the casserole and drape 2 slices of bacon across the breast. Cover the casserole, reduce the heat to its lowest point and simmer the pheasant for about 45 minutes, or until it is tender. (A mature pheasant may take from 15 to 30 minutes longer.) In either case test for doneness by piercing the thigh with the tip of a small, sharp knife. The juice should spurt out a clear yellow. If tinged with pink, simmer for a few minutes longer. Remove the bird to a warm platter and let it rest, loosely covered with foil, while you make the sauce. Discard the bay leaf.

In a 10-inch skillet melt the remaining 2 tablespoons of butter over high heat. When the foam subsides, add the mushrooms and cook for 3 minutes, stirring occasionally. Add the flour and cook, stirring constantly, for a minute or so. With a rubber spatula, transfer the entire contents of the skillet to the casserole. Then stir in the heavy cream and simmer until the sauce thickens slightly. Taste for seasoning. Carve the pheasant into attractive serving pieces, pour the sauce over them and serve at once.

NOTE: In Germany, the pheasant is browned in butter as described above. Because butter alone burns easily, you may prefer to use 2 tablespoons of butter combined with 1 tablespoon of vegetable oil.

Gefüllter Fasan

PHEASANT WITH GIBLET AND CROUTON STUFFING

To serve 4 to 6

STUFFING

3 slices fresh white homemade-type
    bread
2 tablespoons butter
The heart, liver and gizzard of the
    pheasant
4 large chicken livers, about ¼
    pound
1 tablespoon finely chopped parsley

4 whole juniper berries and 3 whole
    black peppercorns, finely
    pulverized with a mortar and pestle
    or wrapped in a towel and crushed
    with a rolling pin
Pinch of ground allspice
Pinch of dried thyme
Pinch of dried marjoram

Preheat the oven to 350°. To make the stuffing, trim off the crusts and cut the bread into ¼-inch cubes. Spread the cubes on a baking sheet and toast in the middle of the oven for 10 minutes, turning them over once or twice. When golden brown, transfer the cubes to a mixing bowl and set aside.

In a heavy 8- to 10-inch skillet, melt 2 tablespoons of butter over moderate heat. When the foam subsides, add the pheasant giblets and the chicken livers, and cook for 2 or 3 minutes, stirring occasionally, until the giblets and liver are lightly browned. Then remove them to a board, chop them very fine and add them to the toasted bread. With a rubber spatula, scrape any fat remaining in the skillet into the bread and stir in the parsley, pulverized juniper berries and pepper, allspice, thyme and marjoram.

PHEASANT

A 3½ to 4-pound oven-ready
    pheasant
3 tablespoons butter, softened
1 tablespoon fresh lemon juice

1 teaspoon salt
4 slices lean bacon
1 cup chicken stock, fresh or canned
½ cup sour cream

Wash the pheasant quickly under cold running water and pat it thoroughly dry inside and out with paper towels. Beat the 3 tablespoons of butter, lemon juice and salt together with a spoon and rub it into the pheasant inside and out. Fill the cavity loosely with the stuffing, and close the opening by lacing it with skewers or sewing it with heavy white thread. Fasten the neck skin to the back of the pheasant with a skewer. Lay the bacon slices side by side across the bird and wrap them around it, pressing the slices snugly against the body to keep them in place.

Place the pheasant, breast side up, on a rack set in a shallow baking pan just large enough to hold the bird comfortably. Roast undisturbed in the middle of the oven for 30 minutes. Then increase the oven heat to 400°, remove the bacon slices and set them aside. Baste the pheasant with ¼ cup of chicken stock and roast for about 30 minutes longer, basting every 10 minutes or so with another ¼ cup of stock. To test for doneness, pierce the thigh of the bird with the tip of a small, sharp knife. The juice should spurt out a clear yellow; if it is slightly pink, roast for another 5 to 10 minutes.

Transfer the pheasant to a heated platter, drape the bacon slices over it, and let the bird rest covered with aluminum foil for 10 minutes before carving. Meanwhile, make the sauce by pouring any remaining stock into the pan, bringing it to a boil over high heat, and scraping in the brown bits clinging to the bottom and sides of the pan. Stir in the sour cream a few tablespoons at a time, and simmer long enough to heat it through. Taste for seasoning. Pour the sauce into a heated sauceboat and serve it with the pheasant.

Dumplings

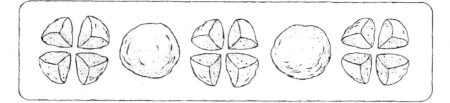

Spätzle

TINY DUMPLINGS

To make about 4 cups

3 cups all-purpose flour
1 teaspoon salt
¼ teaspoon ground nutmeg

4 eggs
1 cup milk
1 cup fine dry bread crumbs
  (optional)
¼ pound (1 stick) butter (optional)

In a large mixing bowl, combine the flour, ½ teaspoon of the salt and the nutmeg. Break up the eggs with a fork and beat them into the flour mixture. Pour in the milk in a thin stream, stirring constantly with a large spoon, and continue to stir until the dough is smooth.

Bring 2 quarts of water and the remaining ½ teaspoon of salt to a boil in a heavy 4- to 5-quart saucepan. Set a large colander, preferably one with large holes, over the saucepan and with a spoon press the dough a few tablespoons at a time through the colander directly into the boiling water. Stir the *Spätzle* gently to prevent them from sticking to each other, then boil briskly for 5 to 8 minutes, or until they are tender. Taste to make sure. Drain the *Spätzle* thoroughly in a sieve or colander. When *Spätzle* are served as a separate dish with roasted meats, such as *Sauerbraten (page 16)*, they are traditionally presented sprinkled with toasted bread crumbs. To toast the crumbs, melt ¼ pound of butter in a heavy 6- to 8-inch skillet over moderate heat. When the foam almost subsides, drop in 1 cup of bread crumbs and cook, stirring constantly, until the crumbs are golden brown.

Kartoffelklösse

POTATO DUMPLINGS

To make 15 to 20 dumplings

½ cup plus 2 tablespoons butter
1 cup fine dry white bread crumbs
2 or 3 slices fresh white homemade-
   type bread, crusts removed
½ cup all-purpose flour
½ cup regular farina, not the quick-
   cooking type

3½ teaspoons salt
⅛ teaspoon ground nutmeg
⅛ teaspoon white pepper
3½ cups hot or cold riced potatoes,
   made from 4 or 5 medium-sized
   baking potatoes (about 1½
   pounds), boiled, peeled and forced
   through a ricer
2 eggs

In a heavy 6- to 8-inch skillet, melt ½ cup of the butter over moderate heat. When the foam begins to subside, drop in the bread crumbs and cook, stirring constantly, until they are light brown. Set the toasted crumbs aside off the heat.

With a small, sharp knife, cut the bread into ½-inch squares (there should be about 1½ cups). Melt the remaining 2 tablespoons of butter in a heavy 8- to 10-inch skillet, add the bread and cook over moderate heat, stirring frequently, until the cubes are light brown on all sides. Add more butter, a tablespoon at a time, if necessary to prevent the bread from burning. Spread the croutons on a double thickness of paper towels to drain.

Combine the flour, farina, 1½ teaspoons of salt, the nutmeg and white pepper in a small bowl. Then, with a large spoon, beat them, a few tablespoons at a time, into the riced potatoes. Lightly beat the two eggs with a fork, and then beat them into the potato mixture. Continue to beat until the dough holds its shape lightly in a spoon. If it seems too thin, stir in a little more flour, a teaspoon at a time until the desired consistency is reached.

Lightly flour your hands and shape each dumpling in the following fashion: Scoop off about 2 tablespoons of dough and form it into a rough ball. Press a hole in the center with a fingertip, drop in 3 or 4 of the reserved croutons, then gather the outer edges of the opening together. Gently roll the dumpling into a ball again.

Bring 4 quarts of water and the remaining 2 teaspoons of salt to a bubbling boil in a deep 6- to 8-quart pot. Drop in all the dumplings, and stir gently once or twice to prevent them from sticking to one another or to the bottom of the pan. Simmer over moderate heat for 12 to 15 minutes, or until the dumplings rise to the surface of the water. Cook 1 minute longer, then remove the dumplings from the pot with a slotted spoon and arrange them on a large heated platter. Serve at once, sprinkled with the reserved toasted bread crumbs.

Kartoffelklösse mit Pflaumenmus
POTATO DESSERT DUMPLINGS WITH PRUNE-BUTTER FILLING

To make 15 dumplings

½ cup butter
¼ cup fine dry white bread crumbs
6 medium-sized boiling potatoes
   (about 2 pounds), scrubbed but
   not peeled
½ cup flour
2 egg yolks
2 teaspoons salt

⅛ teaspoon ground nutmeg
1 tablespoon flour
15 teaspoons prune butter, or
   substitute 15 teaspoons apple
   butter
1 egg white, lightly beaten
¼ cup sugar, or ¼ cup sugar
   combined with ¼ teaspoon
   ground cinnamon

In a heavy 6- to 8-inch skillet, melt the butter over moderate heat. When the foam subsides, add the crumbs and cook, stirring constantly, until they are golden brown. Remove the skillet from the heat and set aside.

Drop the potatoes into enough lightly salted boiling water to cover them completely. Boil briskly for 20 or 30 minutes, or until the potatoes show no resistance when pierced with the point of a small, sharp knife. Drain and peel them, then force them through a ricer set over a mixing bowl. Beat in the ½ cup of flour and the egg yolks one at a time. Add the salt and nutmeg and continue to beat the potatoes, flour and egg yolks until a smooth dough is formed. Taste for seasoning. Refrigerate, covered with plastic wrap or foil, for about one hour.

Sprinkle a large baking sheet with 1 tablespoon of flour, tipping the sheet from side to side to spread the flour evenly. Place the chilled dough on the sheet and with a lightly floured pin roll it out into a rectangle 9 inches wide and 15 inches long. If at any point the dough becomes too sticky to handle, refrigerate it on the sheet until it is firm again.

With a ruler and a pastry wheel or small, sharp knife, measure and cut the dough into 3-inch squares. Drop 1 teaspoon of prune butter into the center of each square and brush all of the edges lightly with the beaten egg white. Fold each of the squares in half diagonally and pinch the edges lightly together to seal them.

Bring 4 quarts of water and 2 teaspoons of salt to a bubbling boil in a wide 6- to 8-quart pot. Drop in 4 or 5 of the dumplings and stir gently once or twice to prevent them from sticking to one another or to the bottom of the pot. Boil briskly for 3 to 4 minutes, until the dumplings rise to the surface, then remove them from the pot with a slotted spoon. As the dumplings are removed from the pot, batch by batch, arrange them side by side on a heated platter, sprinkle them with the reserved toasted bread crumbs and then with the plain sugar or cinnamon sugar. Serve at once.

Dampfnudeln

DESSERT DUMPLINGS WITH VANILLA SAUCE

To make 10 to 12 dumplings

DUMPLINGS
1½ teaspoons active dry yeast (½ envelope)
2 tablespoons sugar
¼ cup lukewarm water (110° to 115°)
¾ cup lukewarm milk (110° to 115°)

2 tablespoons butter, melted
¼ teaspoon salt
2¾ cups sifted all-purpose flour

POACHING LIQUID
2 tablespoons butter
2 tablespoons sugar
½ cup cold milk

In a small, shallow bowl, sprinkle the yeast and 1 tablespoon of the sugar over the ¼ cup of lukewarm water. Let the mixture stand for 2 or 3 minutes, then stir it to dissolve the yeast. Set the bowl in a warm, draft-free place—such as a turned-off oven—for 4 or 5 minutes, or until the yeast bubbles and doubles in volume.

In a mixing bowl, combine the lukewarm milk, melted butter, the remaining 1 tablespoon of sugar, and ¼ teaspoon of salt. Add the yeast and then the flour, beating until a smooth dough is formed. Gather the dough into a ball, and knead it vigorously on a lightly floured surface for about 5 minutes, or until it is smooth and elastic. Then return the dough to the bowl, dust it lightly with flour, and cover with a kitchen towel. Set the dough in a warm, draft-free place for about 45 minutes, or until it has doubled in bulk. Punch the dough down with one blow of your fist. Divide the dough into 10 or 12 equal pieces and with lightly floured hands shape them into balls. Place them 2 inches apart on a baking sheet, and set them aside in the same warm place to double in bulk again. Then, in a heavy 10-inch skillet 2½ inches deep or a flameproof casserole of similar size, melt 2 tablespoons of butter over moderate heat. When the foam subsides, stir in 2 tablespoons of sugar and ½ cup of cold milk. Bring to a boil, then arrange the dumplings side by side in the skillet and cover it tightly. Reduce the heat to low and simmer undisturbed for 15 minutes, or until the dumplings have absorbed all the liquid. Remove from the heat and set the dumplings aside in the covered skillet to keep them warm.

VANILLA SAUCE
4 egg yolks, lightly beaten
½ cup sugar

2 cups cold milk
1 teaspoon vanilla extract

While the dumplings are poaching, make the vanilla sauce. Beat the egg yolks and sugar together with a wire whisk or a rotary or electric beater for 3 or 4 minutes, or until the yolks are thick and pale yellow. Bring 2 cups of cold milk to a boil in a heavy 2- to 3-quart saucepan and then, beating constantly with a whisk, pour the milk in a thin stream over the yolks. Pour the mixture back into the saucepan and cook over low heat, stirring constantly with a spoon, until the sauce is thick enough to coat the spoon lightly. Do not let the sauce come to a boil or it may curdle. Remove the pan from the heat and stir in the vanilla.

To serve, arrange the dumplings, bottom sides up, on a heated platter or individual serving plates and spoon the vanilla sauce over them.

Griessklösse

FARINA DUMPLINGS

To make about 2 dozen dumplings

3 cups milk	1½ cups regular farina, not the quick-cooking type
2½ teaspoons salt	3 eggs
⅛ teaspoon ground nutmeg	Cinnamon-sugar, applesauce, or
3 tablespoons butter	stewed fruit compote *(page 115)*

In a heavy 2- to 3-quart saucepan heat the milk, ½ teaspoon of the salt, the nutmeg and the butter over moderate heat until the butter dissolves and the milk comes to a boil. Pour in the farina slowly, so the milk never stops boiling, stirring it constantly with a wooden spoon. Reduce the heat to low and simmer, stirring frequently, until the farina thickens enough to hold its shape in the spoon. Remove the pan from the heat and beat in the eggs, one at a time. When the farina is cool enough to handle, shape it into round dumplings about 1½ inches in diameter.

Bring 2 quarts of water and 2 teaspoons of salt to a boil in a large saucepan or soup pot and drop in as many dumplings as the pot will hold comfortably. Stir once or twice to prevent the dumplings from sticking to one another or to the bottom of the pan. Reduce the heat to low and simmer, undisturbed, for 15 to 20 minutes. Then, with a slotted spoon, transfer the dumplings to a heated platter. Serve them as a hot dessert, sprinkled with cinnamon-sugar or accompanied by applesauce or stewed fruit *(page 115)*. They may instead be topped with melted butter to accompany a roast or stew. Or they may be made smaller to garnish a soup.

Hefeklösse
YEAST DUMPLINGS

To make 12 dumplings

¼ cup lukewarm water (110° to 115°)

1 package active dry yeast

1 teaspoon sugar

1 egg

4 tablespoons butter, melted and cooled, plus 1 teaspoon butter, softened

¾ cup lukewarm milk (110° to 115°)

1 teaspoon salt

¼ teaspoon ground nutmeg

3½ cups all-purpose flour

Pour the lukewarm water into a small bowl and sprinkle it with the yeast and sugar. Let it stand for 2 or 3 minutes, then stir to dissolve the yeast and sugar completely. Set in a warm, draft-free place (such as a turned-off oven) for about 5 minutes, or until the mixture almost doubles in volume.

In a large mixing bowl, beat the egg with a large spoon until it is smooth and well mixed. Beat in the 4 tablespoons of melted butter, add the warm milk, salt, nutmeg and yeast solution. Then add the flour, ½ cup at a time, beating well after each addition. Mix with the spoon or your hands until the dough is firm enough to be gathered into a compact ball.

Place the dough on a lightly floured surface and knead it by pushing it down with the heels of your hands, pressing it forward and folding it back on itself. Repeat this procedure for about 10 minutes, lightly flouring the surface from time to time to prevent the dough from sticking. When the dough is smooth and elastic, place it in a bowl coated with 1 teaspoon of soft butter, drape it with a towel and let it rise in a warm draft-free place for about 1 hour, or until it doubles in bulk. Then punch the dough down with a sharp blow of your fist and knead it again for 3 or 4 minutes. Flour your hands lightly, pinch off pieces of the dough and shape them into 12 balls about 1½ inches in diameter.

Spread a damp kitchen towel over a rack set in a large roasting pan and on it arrange the dumplings about 2 inches apart. Add enough water to the pan to come to within 1 inch of the rack. Bring to a boil over high heat, cover tightly, and reduce the heat to moderate. Steam the dumplings undisturbed for 20 minutes, or until they are firm to the touch. Serve as hot as possible on a large, heated platter. Traditionally the dumplings are served with meats, or stewed fruit compote *(page 115)*.

Vegetables

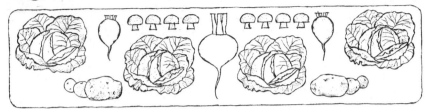

Gedünstetes Sauerkraut
STEAMED SPICED SAUERKRAUT

To serve 4 to 6

2 pounds fresh sauerkraut
1 tablespoon lard
½ cup finely chopped onions
1 tablespoon sugar
2 cups cold water
5 whole juniper berries, 6 whole
  black peppercorns, 2 small bay
leaves, ¼ teaspoon caraway seeds
  (optional) and 1 whole allspice,
  wrapped together in cheesecloth
½ pound boneless smoked pork loin
  or butt, in 1 piece, or substitute
  ½ pound Canadian-style bacon in
  1 piece
1 large raw potato, peeled

Drain the sauerkraut, wash it under cold running water, and let it soak in cold water for 10 to 20 minutes, depending upon its acidity. A handful at a time, squeeze the sauerkraut vigorously until it is completely dry.

In a heavy 3- to 4-quart casserole or saucepan, melt the lard over moderate heat until a light haze forms above it. Add the chopped onions and cook, stirring frequently, for 8 to 10 minutes, or until the onions are light brown. Add the sauerkraut, sugar and 2 cups of water, and mix together thoroughly, separating the strands of sauerkraut with a fork. Bury the bag of spices in the sauerkraut and place the pork or bacon on top of it. Bring to a boil over high heat, then reduce the heat to its lowest point, cover the casserole and cook, undisturbed, for 20 minutes.

Grate the raw potato directly into the casserole, and with a fork stir it into the sauerkraut mixture. Cover the casserole tightly, and cook over low heat for 1½ to 2 hours, or until the sauerkraut has absorbed most of its cooking liquid and the meat is tender when pierced with the tip of a fork. Remove and discard the spices. Taste for seasoning.

To serve, cut the meat into ¼-inch slices. Then transfer the sauerkraut to a large heated platter. Spread the sauerkraut into an even mound and arrange the slices of meat on top.

NOTE: To prepare this as an *Eintopf*, or one-dish meal, which is so popular in Germany, use a 2-pound piece of smoked pork or Canadian-style bacon and cook it as described above. To serve, cut the meat into ¼-inch slices and arrange the slices attractively around the mound of sauerkraut.

Weinkraut

SAUERKRAUT WITH WINE AND GRAPES

To serve 6

2 pounds fresh sauerkraut	2 cups dry white wine
2 tablespoons bacon fat	½ pound seedless green grapes

Drain the sauerkraut, wash it thoroughly under cold running water, and then let it soak in a pot of water for 10 to 20 minutes, depending upon its acidity. A handful at a time, squeeze the sauerkraut until it is completely dry. In a heavy 3-quart casserole or saucepan, heat the bacon fat over moderate heat until a light haze forms above it. Add the sauerkraut and cook for several minutes, separating the strands with a fork. Pour in the wine, and bring it to a boil. Then reduce the heat to its lowest point, cover the casserole, and simmer for 1½ to 2 hours, or until the sauerkraut has absorbed most of the wine. (If at any point during the cooking the sauerkraut seems dry, add a few tablespoons of wine from time to time.) Stir in the grapes, cover the casserole again, and simmer for 10 minutes longer. Serve at once from a heated platter or serving bowl.

Sauerkraut mit Ananas

PINEAPPLE SAUERKRAUT

To serve 6 to 8

2 pounds fresh sauerkraut	(2 twenty-ounce cans)
5 cups unsweetened pineapple juice	A 1½- to 2-pound ripe pineapple

Drain the sauerkraut, wash it thoroughly under cold running water, and let it soak in a pot of cold water for 10 to 20 minutes, depending upon its acidity. A handful at a time, squeeze the sauerkraut until it is completely dry.

Combine the sauerkraut and pineapple juice in a heavy 3- to 4-quart saucepan, and bring to a boil over high heat, stirring with a fork to separate the sauerkraut strands. Reduce the heat to its lowest point and cover the pan tightly. Simmer, undisturbed, for 1½ to 2 hours, or until the sauerkraut has absorbed most of its cooking liquid.

With a long, sharp knife, cut the top 1½ inches off the pineapple and set the top aside. Hollow out the pineapple carefully, leaving a ⅛- to ¼-inch layer of the fruit in the shell. Remove and discard the woody core of the hollowed-out fruit and cut the fruit into ½-inch cubes.

Stir the diced pineapple into the cooked sauerkraut, cook for a minute or two, then pour the entire mixture into a large sieve set over a bowl. When all the liquid has drained through, pile the sauerkraut into the pineapple shell. Cover with the reserved pineapple top and serve on a large plate. If you like, any remaining sauerkraut may be presented mounded on the plate around the pineapple.

Pineapple sauerkraut is traditionally served with roasted smoked pork or with roasted game birds.

Rotkohl mit Äpfeln
RED CABBAGE WITH APPLES

To serve 4 to 6

A 2- to 2½-pound red cabbage
⅔ cup red wine vinegar
2 tablespoons sugar
2 teaspoons salt
2 tablespoons lard or bacon fat
2 medium-sized cooking apples, peeled, cored and cut into

⅛-inch-thick wedges
½ cup finely chopped onions
1 whole onion, peeled and pierced with 2 whole cloves
1 small bay leaf
1 cup boiling water
3 tablespoons dry red wine
3 tablespoons red currant jelly (optional)

Wash the head of cabbage under cold running water, remove the tough outer leaves, and cut the cabbage into quarters. To shred the cabbage, cut out the core and slice the quarters crosswise into ⅛-inch-wide strips.

Drop the cabbage into a large mixing bowl, sprinkle it with the vinegar, sugar and salt, then toss the shreds about with a spoon to coat them evenly with the mixture. In a heavy 4- to 5-quart casserole, melt the lard or bacon fat over moderate heat. Add the apples and chopped onions and cook, stirring frequently, for 5 minutes, or until the apples are lightly browned. Add the cabbage, the whole onion with cloves, and the bay leaf; stir thoroughly and pour in the boiling water. Bring to a boil over high heat, stirring occasionally, and reduce the heat to its lowest possible point. Cover and simmer for 1½ to 2 hours, or until the cabbage is tender. Check from time to time to make sure that the cabbage is moist. If it seems dry, add a tablespoon of boiling water. When the cabbage is done, there should be almost no liquid left in the casserole. Just before serving remove the onion and bay leaf, and stir in the wine and the currant jelly. Taste for seasoning, then transfer the entire contents of the casserole to a heated platter or bowl and serve.

Saure Kartoffeln
SOUR POTATOES

To serve 4 to 6

6 medium-sized boiling potatoes
   (about 2 pounds), peeled and cut
   into ¼-inch slices
2 cups cold water

½ teaspoon salt
½ cup finely chopped lean bacon
2 tablespoons flour
2 tablespoons white wine or cider
   vinegar

In a heavy 3- to 4-quart saucepan, combine the potatoes, water and salt. Bring to a boil over high heat, and boil briskly, uncovered, until the potatoes show no resistance when pierced with the tip of a small, sharp knife. Drain them through a large sieve set over a bowl. Reserve the cooking water and return the potatoes to the pan. Cover the potatoes to keep them warm while you make the sauce.

In a heavy 8-inch skillet cook the bacon over moderate heat until brown and crisp. Stir in the flour, lower the heat and cook, stirring constantly, until the flour browns lightly. Watch carefully for any sign of burning. Slowly pour the reserved cooking water into the skillet, stirring constantly with a spoon. Bring to a boil over high heat, still stirring. When the sauce is smooth and thick, lower the heat and stir in the vinegar. Cover the pan and simmer slowly for 5 minutes. Then pour the sauce over the potatoes, and toss gently with a large spoon to moisten them thoroughly. Taste for seasoning and serve in a heated bowl. Traditionally, sour potatoes accompany sausages of all kinds or cold sliced meats.

Himmel und Erde
POTATOES WITH APPLES

To serve 8

1 tablespoon sugar
2 teaspoons salt
½ teaspoon freshly ground black
   pepper
2 cups cold water
9 medium-sized boiling potatoes
   (about 3 pounds), peeled and cut

into 1-inch cubes
1 pound tart cooking apples, peeled,
   cored and quartered
½ pound lean bacon, cut into ¼-
   inch dice
2 medium-sized onions, peeled and
   sliced ⅛-inch thick and separated
   into rings
1 teaspoon cider vinegar

In a heavy 12-inch skillet combine the sugar, 1 teaspoon of the salt and the black pepper in 2 cups of water. Then drop in the potatoes and apples and bring the water to a boil over high heat. Reduce the heat to moderate and cover the skillet tightly. Simmer, undisturbed, until the potatoes are tender but not falling apart.

Meanwhile, in an 8- to 10-inch skillet, cook the bacon over moderate heat until brown and crisp. With a slotted spoon, spread it out on a double thickness of paper towels to drain. Add the onions to the fat remaining in the skillet and cook over moderate heat, stirring frequently, for 8 to 10 minutes, or until the rings are soft and light brown.

Just before serving, stir the remaining teaspoon of salt and the teaspoon of vinegar into the potatoes and apples, and taste for seasoning. Then transfer the entire contents of the skillet to a heated bowl and serve topped with the onion rings and bacon.

Kartoffelpuffer mit Apfelmus
POTATO PANCAKES WITH APPLESAUCE

To make about 8 pancakes

6 medium-sized potatoes (about 2 pounds), preferably baking potatoes
2 eggs

¼ cup finely grated onion
⅓ cup flour
1 teaspoon salt
Bacon fat or lard
Applesauce or imported lingonberry (*Preiselbeeren*) preserves

Peel the potatoes and as you proceed drop them into cold water to prevent their discoloring. In a large mixing bowl, beat the eggs enough to break them up, add the onion and gradually beat in the flour and salt. One at a time, pat the potatoes dry and grate them coarsely into a sieve or colander. Press each potato down firmly into the sieve to squeeze out as much moisture as possible, then immediately stir it into the egg and onion batter.

Preheat the oven to 250°. In a heavy 8- to 10-inch skillet melt 8 tablespoons of bacon fat or lard over high heat until it splutters. Pour in ⅓ cup of the potato mixture and, with a large spatula, flatten it into a pancake about 5 inches in diameter. Fry it over moderate heat for about 2 minutes on each side. When the pancake is golden brown on both sides and crisp around the edges, transfer it to a heated, ovenproof plate and keep it warm in the oven. Continue making similar pancakes with the remaining batter, adding more fat to the pan when necessary to keep it at a depth of ¼ inch. Serve the pancakes as soon as possible with applesauce or lingonberry preserves.

Grünkohl mit Kartoffeln
BAKED KALE WITH POTATOES

To serve 4 to 6

9 tablespoons butter, softened
3 pounds kale
½ pound lean bacon, coarsely diced
½ cup beef or chicken stock, fresh
  or canned
2 teaspoons salt

¼ teaspoon ground nutmeg
9 medium-sized boiling potatoes
  (about 3 pounds), peeled and cut
  into ½-inch cubes
½ to ¾ cup milk
Freshly ground black pepper
2 egg yolks

With a pastry brush, coat the bottom and sides of an 8-by-10-inch baking dish with 1 tablespoon of softened butter. Set the dish aside.

Wash the kale thoroughly under cold running water. With a small, sharp knife, cut away the ends and the tough stems as well as any bruised or yellowed leaves. Drop the kale into enough lightly salted boiling water to cover it completely and boil briskly for 10 minutes. Drain thoroughly in a colander, and with the back of a spoon press it firmly to remove any excess liquid; then chop the kale coarsely.

In a heavy 4- to 5-quart saucepan, cook the bacon over moderate heat until it is crisp and brown. Add the kale, turning it about with a large spoon until the leaves are coated with the fat. Then stir in the stock, 1 teaspoon of the salt and nutmeg, and bring to a boil over high heat. Reduce the heat to low and simmer uncovered, stirring occasionally, for 20 minutes.

Meanwhile preheat the oven to 400°. Drop the potatoes into enough lightly salted boiling water to cover them completely, and boil them briskly, uncovered, until they are tender but not falling apart. Drain thoroughly, return them to the pan and shake them over low heat for 2 to 3 minutes until they are dry. Then force the potatoes through a food mill or ricer set over a bowl. A tablespoon at a time, beat 6 tablespoons of softened butter into the potatoes and then the milk a few tablespoons at a time, using as much of the milk as you need to make a purée thick enough to hold its shape in a spoon. Beat in the remaining teaspoon of salt, a few grindings of black pepper and the egg yolks, one at a time. Taste for seasoning.

Spread the cooked kale evenly over the bottom of the prepared baking dish, smooth the potatoes over it and dot the top with the remaining 2 tablespoons of butter cut into small pieces. Bake in the middle of the oven for 20 minutes, or until the surface of the potatoes is golden brown. Serve at once, directly from the baking dish.

Hoppelpoppel

EGGS WITH BACON, ONIONS AND POTATOES

To serve 2

3 medium-sized boiling potatoes
  (about 1 pound), unpeeled
1½ cups coarsely diced lean bacon
½ cup finely chopped onions

4 eggs
1 tablespoon milk
2 tablespoons finely chopped parsley
½ teaspoon salt
Freshly ground black pepper

Drop the potatoes into enough lightly salted boiling water to cover them completely. Boil briskly, uncovered, until the potatoes show only the slightest resistance when pierced with the tip of a small, sharp knife. Be careful not to let them overcook.

Meanwhile, in a heavy 10- to 12-inch skillet, cook the bacon over moderate heat until brown and crisp. With a slotted spoon transfer the pieces of bacon to a double thickness of paper towels to drain. Pour all but 2 or 3 tablespoons of fat from the skillet, add the onions, and cook for 5 minutes, stirring them frequently, until they are soft and transparent but not brown. Set the skillet aside.

Drain the potatoes in a colander, then peel and cut them into ¼-inch slices. Add them to the onions in the skillet and cook over moderate heat for 8 to 10 minutes, turning the potatoes occasionally with a large spatula, until they are light brown. Then, in a small bowl, beat the eggs, milk, parsley, salt and a few grindings of pepper together with a fork until they are well blended. Strew the diced bacon over the potatoes and pour in the eggs. Tip the pan from side to side to spread the eggs evenly and cover the skillet. Reduce the heat to low and cook undisturbed for 5 or 6 minutes, shaking the pan gently every now and then to prevent the eggs from sticking. The *Hoppelpoppel* is done when the eggs are set, but still slightly moist. To serve, invert a heated serving plate over the skillet and, grasping skillet and plate firmly together, quickly turn them over. Serve at once.

NOTE: One cup of finely diced cooked ham may be substituted for the bacon. In that case, melt ¼ cup of lard or bacon fat in the skillet and cook the diced ham and the onions together for 5 minutes. Add the sliced potatoes and proceed with the recipe as described above.

Chicorée mit Schinken und Käse
ENDIVE BAKED WITH HAM AND CHEESE

To serve 4

8 large, firm endive, with tightly
    closed, unblemished leaves
1 cup milk
1 cup cold water

1 teaspoon salt
8 thin slices precooked ham, each
    about 4 by 6 inches
8 slices imported Emmentaler or
    Gruyère cheese, cut 4 by 6 inches
    and 1/8 inch thick

With a small, sharp knife trim the base of the endive and wash them under cold running water. (In Germany, part of the bitter center core at the base is sometimes cut out when the endive is trimmed. You may remove about 1/4 inch of the core if you like, but take care not to cut so deeply that the leaves break apart.) Arrange the endive in one layer in a 12-inch stainless-steel or enameled skillet and pour the milk and water over them. Add the salt and heat until small bubbles appear around the rim of the pan. Reduce the heat to low, cover the pan tightly and simmer for 20 minutes, or until the endive are tender but not falling apart. Preheat the oven to 400°. Remove the endive from the pan with tongs and drain them on a double thickness of paper towels. Wrap each one in a slice of ham, then in a slice of cheese. Generously butter a shallow 8-by-10-inch baking dish and arrange the endive rolls in it side by side. Bake undisturbed in the middle of the oven for 10 minutes, or until the cheese softens and has melted. Serve at once, directly from the baking dish.

Pilze mit Tomaten und Speck
MUSHROOMS WITH TOMATOES AND BACON

To serve 4

1 pound fresh mushrooms
2 tablespoons butter
1/2 cup finely diced lean bacon
1/2 cup finely chopped onions
1/2 teaspoon salt

Freshly ground black pepper
3 medium-sized tomatoes, peeled,
    seeded and coarsely chopped
2 tablespoons finely chopped fresh
    parsley

Cut away any tough ends of the mushroom stems. Wipe the mushrooms with a damp paper towel, and cut them, stems and all, into 1/8-inch slices.

In a heavy 10- to 12-inch skillet, melt the butter over moderate heat. When the foam subsides, add the bacon and cook, stirring frequently, until the bacon is crisp and light brown. Add the onions and cook, stirring frequently, for 5 minutes, or until the onions are soft and transparent but not brown. Then drop in the mushrooms and season with salt and a few grind-

68

ings of pepper. Cook over high heat, turning the mushrooms frequently, for 3 or 4 minutes.

When the mushrooms are lightly colored, stir in the chopped tomatoes and simmer over low heat for about 10 minutes.

If there are more than 2 or 3 tablespoons of liquid left in the pan, increase the heat and boil briskly for a minute or so to reduce the excess. Then add the parsley and taste for seasoning. Serve at once from a heated bowl as an accompaniment to meat.

Schmorgurken mit saurem Rahm und Dill
STEWED CUCUMBERS WITH SOUR CREAM AND DILL

To serve 6

	2 cups milk
6 medium-sized firm, fresh	2 tablespoons sour cream
cucumbers (about 3 pounds)	1 tablespoon finely chopped fresh
2 teaspoons salt	parsley
2 tablespoons butter	1 tablespoon finely chopped fresh
½ cup finely chopped onions	dill, or substitute 1 teaspoon dried
2 tablespoons flour	dill weed

With a small, sharp knife, peel the cucumbers and cut them in half lengthwise. Seed them by running the tip of a small spoon down them, from end to end. Cut the cucumber halves crosswise into 1-inch pieces and place them in a large bowl. Sprinkle them with salt, tossing them about with a spoon to spread it evenly. Let the cucumbers stand at room temperature for 30 minutes, then drain off all the liquid and pat them dry with paper towels. In a heavy 10- to 12-inch skillet, melt the butter over moderate heat. When the foam subsides, add the onions and cook, stirring frequently, for 8 to 10 minutes, or until they color lightly. Add the flour and cook, stirring constantly, until the flour turns a golden brown. Watch for any sign of burning and regulate the heat accordingly. Pour in the milk and, stirring constantly, bring to a boil. Reduce the heat to low and simmer for 1 or 2 minutes, until the mixture thickens slightly. Add the cucumbers and simmer, uncovered, for 15 minutes. When the cucumbers are tender but not pulpy, add the sour cream, parsley and dill. Taste for seasoning. Serve in a heated bowl.

Rosenkohl mit Schinken und Tomaten
BRUSSELS SPROUTS WITH HAM AND TOMATOES

To serve 4

2 cups firm fresh Brussels sprouts
2 cups cold water
1½ teaspoons salt
1 cup milk
3 tablespoons butter
4 tablespoons flour
⅛ teaspoon nutmeg
1 cup finely diced cooked ham

(about 6 ounces)
4 medium-sized tomatoes, peeled
and cut into ¼-inch-thick slices
2 tablespoons freshly grated
Parmesan cheese combined with
1 tablespoon fine, dry white bread
crumbs
1 tablespoon butter, cut into small
bits

Preheat the oven to 375°. With a small, sharp knife trim the base of each Brussels sprout and cut off or pull away any wilted or yellowed leaves. Wash the sprouts thoroughly under cold running water. In a heavy 3- to 4-quart saucepan, bring 2 cups of water and 1 teaspoon of the salt to a boil over high heat. Add the Brussels sprouts, and boil gently, uncovered, over moderate heat for 6 to 8 minutes, or until the vegetables are almost but not quite tender when pierced with the tip of a fork. With a slotted spoon, transfer the sprouts to a 1-quart shallow baking dish, and spread them out in one layer. Pour 1 cup of the cooking liquid and the milk into a bowl.

In a 1-quart saucepan, melt 3 tablespoons of butter over moderate heat. When the foam subsides, stir in the flour. Then gradually pour in the milk mixture, and bring to a boil, stirring constantly with a whisk or spoon until the sauce is slightly thickened and smooth. Add the remaining ½ teaspoon of salt and the nutmeg, and taste for seasoning. Scatter the ham evenly over the sprouts, and pour the sauce over them. Top with the sliced tomatoes, placed side by side, and sprinkle them with the cheese and bread-crumb mixture. Dot with bits of butter and bake in the middle of the oven for 20 minutes, or until the sauce bubbles and the top is light brown. Serve at once, directly from the baking dish.

Erbspüree

YELLOW PEA PURÉE WITH BACON

To serve 4 to 6

2 cups dried yellow peas
6 cups water
¼ pound lean bacon in one piece
1 cup finely chopped carrots
1 cup finely chopped celery
1 cup thinly sliced leeks, including

2 inches of the green tops
½ cup finely chopped onions
⅛ teaspoon marjoram
2 tablespoons lard
1 medium-sized onion, peeled and
thinly sliced
3 tablespoons melted butter

Wash the peas thoroughly under cold running water and pick out and discard any blackened ones. In a heavy 4- to 5-quart saucepan, bring the water to a boil over high heat. Add the peas, bacon, carrots, celery, leeks, chopped onions and marjoram, and return to a boil. Reduce the heat to low and simmer, partially covered, for about 45 minutes, or until the peas are soft and have absorbed almost all of the liquid. Remove the bacon and drain it on paper towels. Then purée the peas and vegetables through a food mill or sieve set over a large bowl, and discard any pulp.

With a small, sharp knife, cut the bacon into ½-inch dice. In a heavy 8- to 10-inch skillet, melt the lard over moderate heat, add the bacon and cook, stirring frequently, until the dice are brown and crisp. With a slotted spoon transfer the bacon dice to paper towels to drain, and add the onion rings to the fat remaining in the skillet. Cook over moderate heat, turning the rings frequently, and regulating the heat so that they color evenly on both sides without burning.

Spoon the pea purée into a 2-quart baking dish, spreading it out evenly with a metal spatula. Strew the onion rings over the purée and sprinkle the bacon and then the melted butter on top. Bake in the middle of the oven for 20 minutes, or until the top is golden and lightly crusted. Serve at once, directly from the baking dish.

Westfälisches Blindhuhn
BEANS WITH FRUIT AND VEGETABLES

To serve 4 to 6

1 quart cold water
1 cup dried white beans, preferably
    Great Northern or navy beans
½ pound slab of lean bacon cut
    lengthwise into 3 strips and
    crosswise into halves
1½ pounds cooking apples and 1½
    pounds firm ripe pears, peeled,
    cored and cut into ¼-inch wedges,
    or use 3 pounds of cooking apples,
peeled, cored and cut into
    ¼-inch wedges
1 pound fresh green string beans,
    trimmed, and cut into 2-inch
    lengths
1 cup coarsely diced scraped carrots
3 medium-sized boiling potatoes
    (about 1 pound), peeled and cut
    into ½-inch dice
Salt
Freshly ground black pepper

In a heavy 4- to 6-quart saucepan or soup pot, bring 1 quart of water to a bubbling boil over high heat. Drop in the dried beans and boil uncovered for 2 minutes. Turn off the heat and let the beans soak for 1 hour. Then add the bacon, return the beans to a boil, and reduce the heat to low. Partially cover the pan and simmer as slowly as possible for about 1 hour, or until the beans are barely tender.

Add the apples, pears, green beans, carrots, potatoes, salt to taste and a few grindings of pepper to the beans. Partially cover the pan and simmer, stirring occasionally, for 30 minutes longer, or until the vegetables and fruit are tender and the beans fully cooked. Taste for seasoning and serve hot from a deep heated bowl.

Grüne Sosse

GREEN HERB SAUCE

To make about 1½ cups

½ cup olive oil

2 tablespoons white wine vinegar or fresh lemon juice

1 tablespoon finely chopped fresh chives

1 tablespoon finely chopped fresh sorrel, if available

1 tablespoon finely chopped fresh parsley

1 tablespoon finely chopped watercress

1 tablespoon finely chopped fresh savory, or substitute 1 teaspoon dried savory

1 tablespoon finely chopped fresh dill, or substitute 1 teaspoon dried dill weed

1 tablespoon finely chopped fresh tarragon, or substitute 1 teaspoon dried tarragon

1 tablespoon finely chopped fresh chervil, or substitute 1 teaspoon dried chervil

1 tablespoon finely chopped onion

1 tablespoon finely chopped leek, white part only

¼ teaspoon sugar

½ teaspoon salt

¼ teaspoon freshly ground black pepper

2 hard-cooked eggs, finely chopped

In a mixing bowl, beat the oil and vinegar or lemon juice with a whisk or fork to combine them thoroughly. Then stir in the chives, sorrel, parsley, watercress, savory, dill, tarragon, chervil, onion, leek, sugar, salt and pepper. Gently fold in the chopped eggs and taste for seasoning. Serve at once, or refrigerate tightly covered until ready to use. This sauce is a specialty of Frankfurt and is served traditionally with hot or cold meats.

Salads

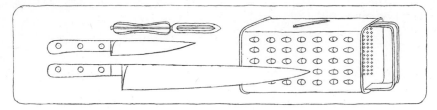

Bohnensalat

GREEN BEAN SALAD

To serve 4

3 tablespoons red or white wine
   vinegar
3 tablespoons olive oil
½ cup chicken stock, fresh or canned
2 teaspoons salt

Freshly ground black pepper
1 teaspoon finely chopped fresh dill
1 teaspoon finely chopped parsley
1 pound fresh green beans
1 sprig fresh summer savory, or ¼
   teaspoon dried summer savory

In a small bowl combine the vinegar, oil, chicken stock, 1 teaspoon of the salt and a few grindings of pepper, and beat them vigorously with a whisk to blend thoroughly. Stir in the dill and parsley, and taste for seasoning. Cover the bowl and set the dressing aside.

With a small, sharp knife, trim the ends off the beans, and cut them into 2-inch lengths. In a 3- to 4-quart saucepan bring 2 quarts of water, the remaining 1 teaspoon of salt and the summer savory to a bubbling boil over high heat. Drop the beans in by the handful. Return the water to a boil, reduce the heat to moderate, and boil the beans, uncovered, for 10 to 15 minutes, or until they are tender but still slightly firm. Do not overcook them. Immediately drain the beans in a colander and run cold water over them for a few seconds to set their color and keep them from cooking further. Spread them out on paper toweling and pat them dry.

Transfer the beans to a large mixing bowl and pour the dressing over them. Stir thoroughly to coat them well, taste for seasoning, and chill for at least 1 hour before serving.

Rote Rübensalat

PICKLED-BEET SALAD

To serve 4

2 pounds fresh firm beets
2 teaspoons salt
½ cup dry red wine
½ cup cider vinegar
1 onion, peeled and thinly sliced
4 whole cloves

½ teaspoon ground coriander seeds
6 whole black peppercorns
3 tablespoons olive oil
1 teaspoon freshly grated
  horseradish, or substitute
  1 tablespoon bottled grated
  horseradish, thoroughly drained
  and squeezed dry in a towel

With a small, sharp knife cut the tops from the beets, leaving about 1 inch of stem on each. Scrub the beets under cold running water, then combine them in a 4- to 5-quart saucepan with enough cold water to cover them by 2 inches. Add 1 teaspoon of the salt and bring the water to a boil over high heat. Reduce the heat to low, cover the pan, and simmer until the beets show no resistance when pierced with the tip of a small, sharp knife. This may take anywhere from 30 minutes for young beets or as long as 2 hours for older ones. The beets should be kept constantly covered with water; add boiling water if necessary.

Drain the beets in a colander and, when they are cool enough to handle, slip off the skins. Cut the beets crosswise into ⅛-inch slices and place them in a deep glass or ceramic bowl.

In a 1½- to 2-quart enameled or stainless-steel saucepan, bring the red wine, vinegar, onion, cloves, coriander, peppercorns and the remaining 1 teaspoon of salt to a boil over high heat. Immediately pour the mixture over the beets. It should cover them completely; if it doesn't, add more wine. Cool to room temperature, cover the bowl tightly with aluminum foil or plastic wrap, and refrigerate for at least 24 hours.

Just before serving, discard the whole cloves and the peppercorns. Beat the olive oil and horseradish together in a small bowl and add it to the beets, turning the slices about with a spoon to coat them thoroughly with the dressing.

NOTE: If you prefer a somewhat thinner dressing, add up to ½ cup of cold water to the oil and horseradish. (Whole canned beets may be substituted for the cooked fresh beets. Slice them ⅛ inch thick and pour the hot marinade over them as described above. Use the canned beet juice in place of water if you wish to dilute the marinade.)

Leichter Kartoffelsalat
SUMMER POTATO SALAD

To serve 4

6 medium-sized boiling potatoes
(about 2 pounds), scrubbed but
not peeled
1 cup finely chopped onions
⅔ cup chicken stock, fresh or
canned
⅓ cup olive oil

1 tablespoon white wine vinegar
2 teaspoons prepared Düsseldorf-
style mustard, or substitute 2
teaspoons other hot, prepared
mustard
2 teaspoons salt
1 teaspoon freshly ground black
pepper
1 tablespoon fresh lemon juice

Drop the unpeeled potatoes into enough lightly salted boiling water to cover them completely. Boil them briskly until they show only the slightest resistance when pierced with the point of a small, sharp knife. Be careful not to let them overcook or they will fall apart when sliced. Drain the potatoes in a colander, then peel and cut them into ¼-inch slices. Set the potatoes aside in a bowl tightly covered with aluminum foil.

In a heavy 2- to 3-quart saucepan, combine the chopped onions, stock, oil, vinegar, prepared mustard, salt and pepper. Bring to a boil over high heat, stirring occasionally. Reduce the heat to low and simmer uncovered for 5 minutes. Remove the pan from the heat and stir in the lemon juice.

Pour the sauce over the potato slices, turning them about with a spatula to coat them evenly. Let the potatoes cool to room temperature, then taste for seasoning and serve.

Warmer Kartoffelsalat mit Speck
HOT POTATO SALAD WITH BACON

To serve 6 to 8

9 medium-sized boiling potatoes
(about 3 pounds), scrubbed but
not peeled
½ pound bacon, finely diced (about
1½ cups)

½ cup finely chopped onions
¼ cup white wine or cider vinegar
¼ cup water
½ teaspoon salt
¼ teaspoon freshly
ground black pepper
2 tablespoons finely chopped parsley

Drop the unpeeled potatoes into enough boiling water to cover them completely. Boil them briskly until they show only the slightest resistance when pierced with the point of a sharp knife. Be careful not to let them overcook or they will fall apart when sliced. Drain the potatoes in a colander, then peel and cut them into ¼-inch slices. Set the potatoes aside in a bowl tightly covered with aluminum foil.

In a heavy 8- to 10-inch skillet, cook the bacon over moderate heat until brown and crisp. Spread it out on paper towels to drain. Add the onions to the fat remaining in the skillet and cook, stirring frequently, for 5 minutes, or until they are soft and transparent but not brown. Stir in the vinegar, water, salt and pepper, and cook, stirring constantly, for a minute or so. Pour the hot sauce over the potatoes, turning the slices about gently with a large spoon or spatula to coat them evenly with the onion-and-vinegar mixture. Gently stir the reserved bacon pieces into the salad. Taste for seasoning.

Serve at once or cover and set the salad aside at room temperature until you are ready to serve it. Just before serving, stir the salad gently and sprinkle the top with parsley.

Selleriesalat mit Äpfeln
CELERY ROOT AND APPLE SALAD

To serve 4

½ cup freshly made mayonnaise, or
  a good, unsweetened commercial
  variety
¼ cup sour cream
1 tablespoon finely chopped fresh
  dill

1 tablespoon finely chopped fresh
  parsley
½ teaspoon salt
Freshly ground black pepper
1 large tart cooking apple, peeled,
  cored and cut into ¼-inch slices
A 1¼- to 1½-pound celery root
  (celeriac)

In a large mixing bowl, beat together the mayonnaise, sour cream, dill, parsley, salt and a few grindings of pepper. Gently stir in the apple slices, cover the bowl and set aside. With a small, sharp knife, peel the celery root and cut it crosswise into ⅛-inch slices. Drop the slices into enough lightly salted boiling water to cover them completely and cook, uncovered, over moderate heat, for 20 to 25 minutes, or until the root shows only the slightest resistance when pierced with the tip of a small, sharp knife. Drain thoroughly and pat the slices completely dry with paper towels. Add the celery root to the dressing and stir gently to coat the slices thoroughly. Taste for seasoning and serve at once, or refrigerate and serve chilled.

Lauchsalat

LEEK SALAD

To serve 4

8 firm fresh leeks, 1 to 1½ inches
   in diameter
¼ cup sour cream
¼ cup cider vinegar
½ teaspoon Düsseldorf-style
   prepared mustard, or substitute

other hot prepared mustard
½ teaspoon freshly grated
   horseradish, or 1 teaspoon
   bottled grated horseradish,
   drained and squeezed dry in a
   towel
½ teaspoon salt
Freshly ground black pepper

With a sharp knife, cut off the roots of the leeks and strip away any withered leaves. Line up the leeks in a row and cut off enough of their green tops to make each leek 6 or 7 inches long. Then slit the green parts in half lengthwise, stopping where they shade into white. Carefully spread the leaves apart and wash the leeks under cold running water to rid them of all sand.

Lay the leeks in 1 or 2 layers in a heavy stainless-steel or enameled skillet or a flameproof casserole just large enough to hold them flat. Pour in enough cold water to cover them and bring to a boil over high heat. Reduce the heat to low, and simmer gently for 10 minutes, or until the leeks show only the slightest resistance when pierced with a fork. Do not overcook.

With tongs or a slotted spoon, transfer the leeks to a double layer of paper towels and let them drain for a minute or two. Then arrange the leeks in a serving dish or deep platter just large enough to hold them. In a small bowl, combine ¼ cup of the leek cooking liquid with the sour cream, vinegar, mustard, horseradish, salt and a few grindings of black pepper. Beat the mixture with a whisk or spoon until it is well blended, and taste for seasoning. Pour the dressing over the leeks. Cool to room temperature, then refrigerate the leeks for about an hour, or until chilled.

Breads and Cookies

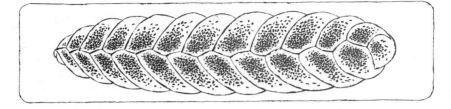

Dresdner Stollen

DRESDEN CHRISTMAS FRUIT BREAD

To make two 13-inch loaves

½ cup seedless raisins
½ cup dried currants
1 cup mixed candied citrus peel
¼ cup candied angelica, cut into ¼-inch dice
½ cup candied cherries, cut in half
½ cup rum
¼ cup lukewarm water (110° to 115°)
2 packages active dry yeast
¾ cup plus a pinch of sugar

5½ cups plus 2 tablespoons all-purpose flour
1 cup milk
½ teaspoon salt
½ teaspoon almond extract
½ teaspoon finely grated fresh lemon peel
2 eggs, at room temperature
¾ cup unsalted butter, cut into ¼-inch bits and softened
8 tablespoons melted unsalted butter
1 cup blanched slivered almonds
¼ cup confectioners' sugar, sifted

Combine the raisins, currants, candied citrus peel, angelica and cherries in a bowl. Pour the rum over them, tossing the fruit about to coat the pieces evenly. Soak for at least 1 hour.

Pour the lukewarm water into a small bowl and sprinkle it with the yeast and a pinch of sugar. Let the mixture stand for 2 or 3 minutes, then stir to dissolve the yeast completely. Set the bowl in a warm, draft-free place (such as a turned-off oven) for about 5 minutes, or until the mixture almost doubles in volume.

Meanwhile, drain the fruit, reserving the rum, and carefully pat the pieces completely dry with paper towels. Place the fruit in a bowl, sprinkle it with 2 tablespoons of the flour, and turn it about with a spoon until the flour is completely absorbed. Set aside.

In a heavy 1½- to 2-quart saucepan, combine the milk, ½ cup of the sugar and the salt. Heat to lukewarm (110° to 115°), stirring constantly until the sugar dissolves. Off the heat, stir in the reserved rum, the almond extract and fresh lemon peel, and finally the yeast mixture.

Place 5 cups of the flour in a large bowl and with a fork stir in the yeast mixture, a cup or so at a time. Beat the eggs until frothy and stir them into the

Continued on next page

dough, then beat in the bits of softened butter. Gather the dough into a ball and place it on a board sprinkled with the remaining ½ cup of flour. Knead the dough, by pushing it down with the heels of your hands, pressing it forward and folding it back on itself. Continue the kneading for about 15 minutes, or until all the flour is incorporated and the dough is smooth and elastic. Flour your hands lightly from time to time. Now press the fruit and almonds into the dough, ⅓ cup or so at a time, but do not knead or handle it too much or the dough will discolor. Coat a deep bowl with 1 teaspoon of melted butter and drop in the dough. Brush the top of the dough with another 2 teaspoons of melted butter, drape a towel over the bowl and set it in a warm, draft-free place for 2 hours, or until the dough doubles in bulk.

Punch the dough down and divide it into two equal pieces. Let them rest for 10 minutes, then roll the pieces out into strips about 12 inches long, 8 inches wide and ½ inch thick. Brush each strip with 2 tablespoons of the remaining butter and sprinkle each with 2 tablespoons of the remaining sugar. Fold each strip lengthwise in the following fashion: bring one long side over to the center of the strip and press the edge down lightly. Then fold the other long side across it, overlapping the seam down the center by about 1 inch. Press the edge gently to keep it in place. With lightly floured hands, taper the ends of the loaf slightly and pat the sides gently together to mound it in the center. The finished loaf should be about 3½ to 4 inches wide and 13 inches long.

With a pastry brush, and 1 tablespoon of melted butter, coat the bottom of an 11-by-17-inch jelly-roll pan. Place the loaves on the pan and brush them with the remaining 2 tablespoons of melted butter. Set the loaves aside in a warm draft-free place for about 1 hour, or until doubled in bulk. Preheat the oven to 375°. Then bake the bread in the middle of the oven for 45 minutes, or until golden brown and crusty. Transfer the loaves to wire racks to cool completely. Just before serving, sprinkle the loaves with the sifted confectioners' sugar.

Weissbrot mit Kümmel
WHITE BREAD WITH CARAWAY SEEDS

To make one 10-inch round loaf

¼ cup lukewarm water (110° to 115°)
3 packages active dry yeast
2 teaspoons sugar
½ cup lukewarm milk (110° to 115°)

4 cups sifted all-purpose flour
2 eggs, at room temperature
¼ pound unsalted butter, cut into ¼-inch pieces and softened to room temperature
1 tablespoon salt
1 tablespoon caraway seeds
Cornmeal

Pour the lukewarm water into a small, shallow bowl and sprinkle the yeast and ½ teaspoon of the sugar over it. Let the yeast and sugar stand 2 or 3 minutes, then stir together to dissolve them completely. Set in a warm, draft-free place, such as an unlighted oven, for 3 to 5 minutes, or until the mixture almost doubles in volume.

Transfer the yeast to a large mixing bowl and stir in the milk. Beat in 3 cups of the sifted flour about ¼ cup at a time. Then beat in the eggs one at a time, and finally beat in the bits of butter. Continue to beat until the dough can be gathered into a compact ball.

Place the ball on a lightly floured board and knead in the remaining cup of flour, a few tablespoons at a time, pushing the dough down with the heels of your hands, pressing it forward and folding it back on itself. Knead until all the flour is incorporated and the dough is stiff and quite dry. Shape it into a rough ball, place it in a mixing bowl, and add enough cold water to cover it by several inches. In 10 to 15 minutes, the top of the dough should rise above the surface of the water.

Remove the dough from the water and pat the surface as dry as you can with paper towels. Return it to a floured board, punch it down, and sprinkle with the remaining 1½ teaspoons of sugar, the salt and the caraway seeds. Lightly flouring the dough from time to time, knead it for about 10 minutes, or until smooth and elastic. Pat and shape the dough into a round loaf about 8 inches in diameter, mounded slightly in the center.

Sprinkle a baking sheet lightly with cornmeal, place the dough in the center of the sheet and cover it loosely with a kitchen towel. Let the dough rise in a warm draft-free place for about 30 minutes, or until it doubles in bulk. Preheat the oven to 375°.

Bake the bread in the middle of the preheated oven for about 1 hour. The crust should be a light golden color. Remove the bread from the baking sheet and cool it on a rack before serving.

Spritzgebäck
PRESSED HAZELNUT COOKIES

To make about 5 dozen cookies

½ pound butter (2 sticks), softened
1 cup sugar
2 eggs

1 teaspoon vanilla extract
2 cups sifted all-purpose flour
1 cup shelled hazelnuts, pulverized
   in an electric blender or with a
   nut grinder or mortar and pestle

Preheat the oven to 350°. In a large bowl, cream the butter and sugar together by mashing them against the sides of the bowl with a large spoon until light and fluffy. Then beat in the eggs one at a time, add the vanilla and continue beating until smooth. Sift the flour into the mixture ½ cup at a time, beating well after each addition. Finally, beat in the ground nuts.

Place the dough in a pastry bag or cookie press fitted with a medium-sized star tip. Pipe the dough out on ungreased baking sheets forming rounds and rings about 1½ inches in diameter, or S-shapes and crescents about 2 inches long, and spacing the cookies 1 inch apart. Bake in the middle of the oven for about 10 minutes, or until the cookies are firm and light brown. With a spatula, transfer them immediately to a cake rack to cool. The *Spritzgebäck* can be stored for several weeks in tightly sealed jars or tins.

Haselnussmakronen
HAZELNUT MACAROONS

To make about 20 cookies

2 teaspoons butter, softened
2 egg whites
¾ cup sugar
1½ cups shelled hazelnuts
   (preferably blanched), pulverized

   in an electric blender or with a
   nut grinder or mortar and pestle
6 tablespoons unsweetened cocoa
2 teaspoons finely grated lemon peel
A pinch of salt
1 teaspoon vanilla extract

With a pastry brush or paper towel, coat a large baking sheet with 2 teaspoons of soft butter and set it aside. In a large bowl, beat the egg whites with a wire whisk or a rotary or electric beater until they foam and thicken slightly. Sprinkle the sugar over them and continue to beat until the whites form stiff, unwavering peaks on the beater when it is lifted out of the bowl. Combine the ground hazelnuts, cocoa, lemon peel, salt and vanilla in a small bowl and, with a rubber spatula, gently but thoroughly fold the mixture into the whites, using an over-under cutting motion rather than a stirring motion. To make the cookies, drop the dough by the tablespoon onto the prepared baking sheet, spacing them about an inch apart. Let the cookies rest at room temperature for 1 hour before baking.

Preheat the oven to 300°. Bake the cookies in the middle of the oven for 30 minutes, or until they are firm. With a spatula, carefully transfer the cookies to a cake rack to cool. *Haselnussmakronen* can be stored for several weeks in tightly sealed jars or tins.

S-Gebäck

S-SHAPED BUTTER COOKIES

To make about 7 dozen cookies	7 egg yolks
	1 teaspoon finely grated lemon peel
½ pound (2 sticks) plus 2 teaspoons unsalted butter, softened	4 cups all-purpose flour
	1 egg white
1 cup sugar	Decorating sugar

In a large bowl, cream the ½ pound of butter and the cup of sugar together by mashing and beating them against the sides of the bowl with a large spoon until light and fluffy. Then beat in the egg yolks one at a time, add the lemon peel and continue beating until smooth. Sift the flour into the mixture, ½ cup at a time, beating well after each addition.

Pat and shape the dough into a long roll about 2 inches in diameter, wrap it in wax paper, and refrigerate it for at least 30 minutes, or until firm.

Preheat the oven to 400°. With a pastry brush and the remaining 2 teaspoons of soft butter, lightly coat two large baking sheets. Set aside. Slice the dough into rounds about ⅓ inch thick. To shape each cookie, roll a slice of dough between your hands to form a rope about ½ inch thick and 4 to 5 inches long. Gently press the rope flat on a pastry board to make a strip about ¾ inch wide and ¼ inch thick. Then with your fingers, form the strip into an S shape. Arrange the cookies an inch apart on the baking sheets and refrigerate for 10 minutes.

In a large bowl, beat the egg white with a whisk or a rotary or electric beater until it is frothy and lightly thickened. Brush the top of each cookie lightly with the white and sprinkle it with a little of the decorating sugar. Bake in the middle of the oven for about 10 minutes, or until the cookie is firm but only faintly colored. With a spatula, transfer the cookies to cake racks to cool. *S-Gebäck* can be stored for several weeks in tightly sealed jars or tins.

To make chocolate pretzels, shape the dough into a roll 2 inches in diameter, then slice it into rounds about ⅜ inch thick (*recipe below*). Roll each round between your hands to make a ¼-inch rope about 14 inches long. Drape the rope on a board into a loop with its ends crossed so that it looks like a small script "e" (*left*). Twist the ends of rope again under the loop (*center*). Spread the tips apart, bring the loop over to them and pinch the tips to the loop (*right*).

Schokoladen Brezeln
CHOCOLATE PRETZELS

To make 25 pretzels

¼ pound (1 stick) unsalted butter, softened
¼ cup sugar

¼ cup unsweetened cocoa
3 tablespoons hot water
2 cups all-purpose flour
1 egg, lightly beaten
1 teaspoon vanilla extract

In a large mixing bowl, cream the butter and ¼ cup of sugar together by beating and mashing them against the sides of the bowl with a large spoon until light and fluffy. Dissolve the cocoa in the hot water, let it cool to room temperature, and beat it into the butter-sugar mixture. Then beat in the flour, a cup at a time, and when it has all been absorbed, add the egg and vanilla. Pat and shape the dough into a cylinder about 7 inches long and 2 inches in diameter. Wrap in wax paper and refrigerate for 30 minutes, or until firm.

Preheat the oven to 350°. Slice the dough crosswise into ⅜-inch rounds and roll each slice between your hands to make a rope-like strip about 14 inches long and ¼ inch in diameter. Shape each rope into a pretzel as shown above. Arrange the pretzels 1 inch apart on ungreased baking sheets and bake in the middle of the oven for 10 minutes, or until they are firm to the touch. Transfer the pretzels to a cake rack to cool.

GLAZE
½ cup milk
⅔ cup sugar
2 ounces sweet chocolate

2 ounces unsweetened
  chocolate
½ cup light corn syrup
1 teaspoon butter

To make the glaze, combine the milk, ⅔ cup of sugar, sweet chocolate, unsweetened chocolate and corn syrup in a small, heavy saucepan or the top of a double boiler. Cook over low heat or simmering water, stirring constantly, until the sugar is dissolved and the chocolate melted. Stir in 1 teaspoon of butter, remove the pan from the heat and cool to lukewarm. With tongs, dip the pretzels into the glaze one at a time to coat them thoroughly. Dry them for at least 15 minutes on a cake rack set over wax paper.

Pfeffernüsse
SPICE COOKIES

To make about 30 cookies

Soft butter
4 cups all-purpose flour
1 teaspoon double-acting baking
  powder
1 teaspoon ground cloves

½ teaspoon ground allspice
½ teaspoon ground cinnamon
¾ cup honey
1 cup dark corn syrup
¾ cup sugar
2 tablespoons butter
1 tablespoon lard

Preheat the oven to 400°. Coat two large baking sheets lightly with butter. Combine the flour, baking powder, cloves, allspice and cinnamon in a bowl, and set aside. In a deep, heavy 5- to 6-quart saucepan, bring the honey, corn syrup and sugar to a boil over moderate heat, stirring until the sugar dissolves. Reduce the heat to low and simmer, uncovered, for 5 minutes. Remove the pan from the heat, add the butter and lard, and stir until melted. Beat in the flour mixture, a cup or so at a time. When the batter is smooth, drop it by teaspoonfuls onto the baking sheets, leaving an inch or so between the cookies. Bake in the middle of the oven for about 15 minutes, or until the cookies are firm to the touch and light brown. Transfer them to a cake rack to cool, and proceed with the remaining batches, coating the baking sheets with a little butter each time. If you like, you may brush the cookies while still warm with the almond glaze for *Honigkuchen (page 88). Pfeffernüsse* can be stored for 6 to 8 weeks in tightly sealed jars or tins.

Mandel-Halbmonde

ALMOND CRESCENT COOKIES

To make about 3 dozen

TOPPING

¼ cup blanched almonds, finely chopped

⅓ cup sugar
1 teaspoon ground cinnamon

Stir the chopped almonds, the ⅓ cup of sugar and the cinnamon together in a small bowl and set aside. Preheat the oven to 325°.

COOKIES

½ pound (2 sticks) unsalted butter, softened
¾ cup sugar
4 hard-cooked egg yolks, sieved

2 raw egg yolks
2 teaspoons finely grated lemon peel
3 cups all-purpose flour, sifted before measuring
1 egg white

In an electric mixer, beat the butter and the ¾ cup of sugar together at high speed until the mixture is light and fluffy. Then beat in the hard-cooked egg yolks, raw egg yolks and lemon peel. Reduce the speed to medium and sift in the flour, beating until the mixture is smooth. (To make the dough by hand, cream the butter and sugar together by mashing and beating them against the sides of the bowl with a large spoon until light and fluffy. Then beat in the hard-cooked egg yolks, raw yolks and lemon peel, and continue to beat until smooth. Sift the flour into the mixture a little at a time, beating well after each addition.)

In a small bowl, beat the egg white with a whisk or a rotary or electric beater until it is stiff enough to form unwavering peaks on the beater when it is lifted out of the bowl. Shape each cookie in the following fashion: Pinch off about 2 tablespoons of dough and roll it between the palms of your hands to make a cylinder about 2½ inches long. Curve the ends of the cylinder together, flatten it a little and taper the ends to form a crescent. Then dip the crescent into egg white and roll it in the almond mixture. Place the cookie on an ungreased baking sheet. Make the remaining cookies similarly, arranging them on the sheet 1 inch apart. (Use 2 baking sheets if necessary.)

Bake in the middle of the oven for about 10 minutes, or until the cookies are firm. With a metal spatula, transfer to cake racks to cool. *Mandel-Halbmonde* can be stored for several weeks in tightly sealed jars or tins.

Springerle

MOLDED ANISE-SEED COOKIES

To make 2 to 3 dozen cookies,
depending on size of forms used

2 tablespoons butter, softened
1 cup anise seeds

2 eggs
1¼ cups sugar
1 teaspoon finely grated lemon peel
A drop of vanilla extract
3 cups sifted all-purpose flour

With a pastry brush or paper towel, coat two large baking sheets with a tablespoon of butter each. Sprinkle the butter evenly with the anise seeds and set the pans aside.

In a large bowl, beat the eggs with a whisk or a rotary or electric beater until they are thick and lemon-colored. Gradually add the sugar and continue beating until the mixture is thick enough to fall back on itself in a slowly dissolving ribbon when the beater is lifted from the bowl. Beat in the lemon peel and vanilla, and then the flour, a cup or so at a time.

Shape the dough into a ball and place it on a lightly floured board. If it feels sticky, work additional flour into it with your fingers, adding a tablespoon at a time. Then knead the dough with lightly floured hands for 10 minutes or so, until it is smooth and pliable.

Sprinkle the board with flour again, pinch off about half of the dough and roll it out into a rectangle about ¼ inch thick. Sprinkle a *Springerle* mold or *Springerle* rolling pin evenly with 2 tablespoons of flour, and rap it sharply on a table to remove the excess. Then press the mold down or roll the pin firmly across the dough, to print the pattern on it as deeply and clearly as possible. Cut the cookie squares apart with a small, sharp knife and place them an inch apart on the prepared baking sheets, pressing them gently into the anise seeds. Roll and cut the rest of the dough similarly. You must work quickly because the dough dries rapidly. Set the cookies aside uncovered at room temperature for 24 hours.

Preheat the oven to 250° and bake the cookies for 20 to 30 minutes, or until they are firm but not brown. With a large metal spatula, transfer the cookies to a cake rack to cool. Then set them aside uncovered for a few days to soften. They may be stored for several weeks in tightly sealed jars or tins.

NOTE: Save the anise seeds remaining on the baking sheets and scatter them over the bottom of the cookie jar or tin. Their flavor will permeate the cookies as they stand.

Honigkuchen

HONEY CAKE

To make one 11-by-17-inch cake

1 cup blanched slivered almonds
(optional)

ALMOND GLAZE (OPTIONAL)

1 cup confectioners' sugar
½ teaspoon almond extract
1 teaspoon fresh lemon juice, or 1
teaspoon rum
2 tablespoons cold water

Preheat the oven to 350°. If you would like to top the cake with nuts, spread the 1 cup of slivered almonds evenly over a baking sheet or in a large, shallow baking dish and toast them in the oven, stirring and turning them frequently, for about 10 minutes, or until they are light brown. Watch carefully for signs of burning. Set aside.

If you would prefer to glaze the cake instead of covering it with almonds, prepare the glaze by stirring the confectioners' sugar, almond extract and lemon juice or rum together in a small bowl. Stirring constantly, add about 2 tablespoons of cold water, 1 teaspoon at a time, until the glaze is smooth and thin enough to be spread easily.

CAKE

1 tablespoon butter, softened
5 cups plus 2 tablespoons all-purpose
flour
1½ teaspoons double-acting baking
powder
¼ cup blanched almonds, pulverized
in an electric blender or with a
nut grinder or a mortar and pestle
3 tablespoons finely chopped candied
citron

1 tablespoon unsweetened cocoa
1 teaspoon ground cloves
1 teaspoon ground cinnamon
2 teaspoons ground cardamom
1 teaspoon finely grated lemon peel
½ teaspoon almond extract
1 cup honey
1 cup sugar
½ cup cold water

With a pastry brush or paper towel, coat the bottom and sides of an 11-by-17-inch jelly-roll pan with the 1 tablespoon of soft butter. Sprinkle 2 tablespoons of the flour over the butter and tip the pan from side to side to spread it evenly. Then invert the pan and rap the bottom sharply to remove any excess flour. Set aside.

In a large bowl, stir together the 5 cups of flour, baking powder, ground almonds, chopped citron, cocoa, cloves, cinnamon, cardamom, lemon peel and almond extract. In a heavy 5-quart saucepan or casserole, bring the honey, sugar and water to a boil over moderate heat, stirring only until the sugar dissolves. Reduce the heat to low and simmer, uncovered, for 5 minutes. Pour the hot honey mixture over the flour mixture and beat them together with a large spoon until a smooth dough is formed.

With your fingers, pat and spread the dough out evenly in the prepared pan. Bake in the middle of the oven for 20 minutes, or until top is firm to the touch. Remove the pan from the oven and, if you are using almonds, strew them over the cake immediately, pressing them gently into the surface. Let the cake rest for 4 or 5 minutes, then cut it into rectangles or fancy shapes of whatever size you like and transfer the pieces to a wire rack to cool. If glazing the cake, brush the top with almond glaze before it is cut.

Honigkuchen should be wrapped in foil or placed in a cookie jar or tin and allowed to mellow for several days before it is served. It can be kept in a tightly covered jar for 2 or 3 months.

Lebkuchen
SPICED HONEY COOKIES

To make 2 to 3 dozen cookies,
   depending on size

2 tablespoons butter, softened
2¼ cups plus 2 tablespoons flour
½ teaspoon double-acting baking
   powder
½ teaspoon ground cloves
½ teaspoon ground cinnamon
¼ teaspoon ground nutmeg
1 cup shelled almonds, ground in

an electric blender or with a nut
   grinder or a mortar and pestle
2 tablespoons finely chopped
   candied orange peel
2 tablespoons finely chopped candied
   lemon peel
2 eggs
½ cup sugar
1 cup honey
½ cup milk
Almond glaze *(see Pfeffernüsse, page 85)*

Lightly coat the bottom and sides of an 11-by-17-inch jelly-roll pan with the soft butter. Sprinkle 2 tablespoons of flour evenly over the butter and tip the pan from side to side to coat the surface evenly. Then invert the pan, and rap it sharply on a table to remove any excess flour. Set aside. Preheat the oven to 400°.

Sift the 2¼ cups flour, baking powder, cloves, cinnamon and nutmeg into a large bowl, and stir in the almonds, orange peel and lemon peel. With a whisk or a rotary or electric beater, beat the eggs and sugar together until the mixture is thick enough to fall back on itself in a slowly dissolving ribbon when the beater is lifted from the bowl. Beat in the honey, then the milk, and finally, a little at a time, the flour mixture. When the batter is smooth, spread it out evenly in the jelly-roll pan with a rubber spatula. Bake in the middle of the oven for 12 to 15 minutes, or until the cake is firm to the touch.

With a knife or metal spatula, loosen the sides of the cake from the pan and turn it out on a cake rack. While it is still warm, brush the top with a thin coating of the glaze, let it set for a minute or so, then cut the cake into cookies 2½ inches long and 1½ inches wide. *Lebkuchen* can be stored for 6 to 8 weeks in tightly sealed jars or tins.

Lebkuchen Häuschen

GINGERBREAD HOUSE

GINGERBREAD
1 tablespoon butter, softened
6¼ cups all-purpose flour
6 tablespoons double-acting baking
  powder
1½ teaspoons ground cinnamon
1 teaspoon ground cloves
¼ teaspoon ground nutmeg
¼ teaspoon ground cardamom

⅛ teaspoon salt
¾ cup honey
1¾ cups sugar
¼ cup butter
⅓ cup fresh lemon juice
1 tablespoon finely grated lemon
  peel
1 egg
1 egg yolk

NOTE: This recipe makes enough dough for one 11-by-17-inch gingerbread cake. You will need three of these cakes to make the house shown on the cover and in the diagrams on pages 92 and 93. You may bake the cakes in three batches (they become firmer and easier to handle as they age, so it is possible to do the baking over a period of several days as long as you cut them as soon as they are baked). Or you may double or triple this recipe and make the cakes in one or two batches; in that event, you will need a very large mixing bowl and extra pans. The icing recipe is intended to make enough for the whole house, but generous decorations may require more.

Cut out the cardboard templates for the house and its base as shown in the diagrams on page 92. Set them aside. With a pastry brush or paper towel, lightly coat an 11-by-17-inch jelly-roll pan with 1 tablespoon of soft butter. Sprinkle ¼ cup of flour into the pan, and tip it from side to side to coat it evenly. Then turn it over and knock out the excess. Set the pan aside.

Sift 6 cups of flour, baking powder, cinnamon, cloves, nutmeg, cardamom and salt together into a large mixing bowl and set them aside.

Preheat the oven to 325°. In a heavy 4- to 5-quart saucepan, bring the honey, sugar and butter to a boil over high heat, stirring with a large spoon until the sugar is dissolved and the butter melted. Remove the pan from the heat, mix in the lemon juice and lemon peel, and cool to room temperature. Beat in 2 cups of the flour-and-spice mixture, add the egg and egg yolk, and then beat in the remaining 4 cups of flour-and-spice mixture. Flour your hands lightly and knead until the dough is smooth, pliable and still slightly sticky. If it is too moist to handle, beat in more flour by the tablespoon.

Place the dough in the jelly-roll pan, and with a lightly floured pin, press and roll it out as evenly as possible, forcing it into the corners with your fingers. Bake for 35 minutes, or until the cake is firm and the top brown. Let the cake cool in the pan for 4 or 5 minutes, then using the templates as your guide, cut it into the requisite shapes with a pastry wheel or small knife. Do not be tempted to cut the house pieces freehand; they must fit together precisely to make a stable structure. Set the pieces aside on wax paper until they cool completely. Bake and cut the remaining cakes in the same fashion.

DECORATION

2 egg whites
2½ cups confectioners' sugar
Candies and cookies for decorating

the house
1 to 2 cups sugar for decorating the base

In a large bowl, beat the egg whites with a whisk or a rotary or electric beater until they are frothy and slightly thickened. Sift the confectioners' sugar into the whites ½ cup at a time, beating thoroughly after each addition. Continue to beat for about 3 minutes, or until a stiff icing is formed. Fill a pastry bag fitted with a round decorative tip with a cup of the icing.

While the pieces of gingerbread are still spread out flat, decorate the front, back and sides of the house with windows, shutters, doors and the like to approximate the gingerbread house shown on the cover, or to suit your own fancy. When the icing is completely dry, assemble the base and walls of the house according to the directions on page 93, using the icing as cement to hold the pieces together. Let the walls stand undisturbed until the icing is completely set. With the remaining icing, cement the roof and chimney pieces in place, and after the icing is set, decorate the roof and chimney. Make more icing if necessary. For more elaborate decoration, coat candies and cookies on one side with the icing and press them gently onto the walls and roof. As a final touch, sift a snowlike coating of sugar over the base.

A Gingerbread House That Can Stand for Years

A gingerbread house like the one on the cover is as much fun to make as it is to look at, and you may be as whimsical as you like with its decoration. But to make a house that will stand proudly through the Christmas holidays for years to come, the gingerbread must be cut with precision and all of the pieces fitted firmly together.

The first step is to make patterns for the pieces from stiff cardboard, following the dimensions and shapes in the diagrams at right. (Where pieces are identical, one pattern will do.) Now bake three 11-by-17-inch gingerbread cakes according to the recipe on page 90. While the cakes are still in the pans, lay the patterns on the cakes and cut the warm gingerbread with a pastry wheel or a small, sharp knife. If you like, cut out a door and a window or two as well. With a wide metal spatula, slide the cakes onto wax paper to cool. (There will be gingerbread left over, including one piece big enough to be cut into gingerbread figures.) Then outline door and window frames, shutters and other trim on the walls with the egg-white-and-sugar icing described on page 91.

After the wall trim decorations are dry, set the base on a cutting board or a large piece of heavy cardboard to enable you to move the house from place to place when it is finished. Assemble the house, using icing to cement the pieces together.

First ice the bottom of one end wall—the back of the house—and the bottom and one end of a side wall; fit them together and place them carefully on the base. Ice the bottom and two sides of a corner post and place it between them. Hold the pieces upright for 3 or 4 minutes, until the icing has set. Ice the opposite end of the side wall and the bottom of the other end wall, and fit that wall onto the house for

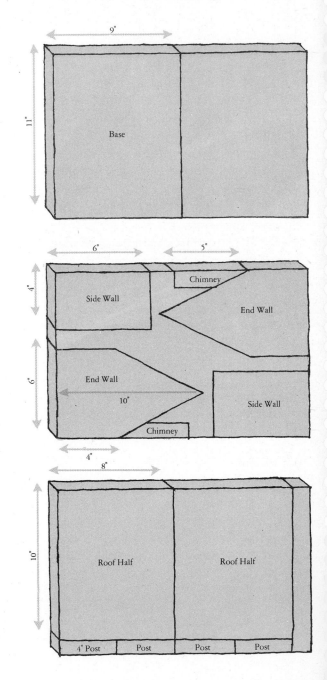

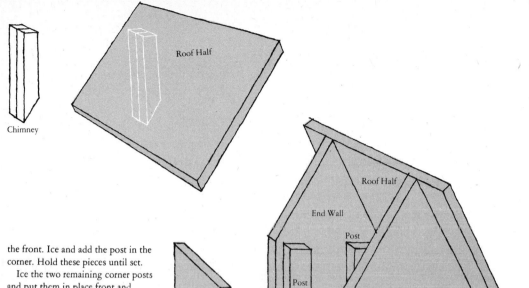

Chimney

Roof Half

Roof Half

End Wall

Post

Side Wall

Post

End Wall

Base

the front. Ice and add the post in the corner. Hold these pieces until set.

Ice the two remaining corner posts and put them in place front and back, allowing space for the side wall as shown in the exploded view of the house, top right. Now ice the bottom and ends of the remaining wall and put it into place. Hold the wall until it is set, then let the icing dry for at least 10 minutes.

Finally, ice the top edges of the end walls and lay the roof over them. The roof pieces should meet, but do not try to overlap them; simply fill the space between them with icing to make a roof peak. Hold the roof until it is steady. Then ice and join the two chimney parts, ice the bottom and put the chimney in place, holding it until it sets.

Decorate the house as fancifully as you like with icing and with candies and cookies. (If you need more icing, make another batch.) Apply the roof icing first, forcing it through a pastry bag or swirling it on with a small metal spatula. Don't forget a crown of icing snow for the chimney top. Spread the candies and cookies with icing and press them gently into place. When the house is done to your taste, sprinkle the roof and base with snowdrifts of sugar.

Fragile though it seems, the finished house can be a delight for many Christmases. Just cover it well with plastic wrap and store it in a cool dry place between seasons.

Heidesand
BROWN BUTTER COOKIES

To make about 3 dozen cookies

1 tablespoon butter, softened
12 tablespoons unsalted butter
1 teaspoon vanilla extract

2 cups all-purpose flour
1 teaspoon double-acting baking
  powder
½ cup sugar

With a pastry brush or paper towel, lightly coat one large or two small baking sheets with the tablespoon of soft butter and set aside.

In a heavy 3- to 4-quart saucepan, melt the 12 tablespoons of butter over low heat and let it cook until it browns slightly. Be careful not to let it burn. Pour the butter into a large mixing bowl and let it cool to room temperature. Then stir in the vanilla. Sift the flour, baking powder and sugar gradually into the butter, stirring as you proceed. With your hands mix the dough until it is smooth and can be formed into a compact ball. Place it on a board. Then pat and shape it into a long roll about 1½ inches in diameter, wrap it in wax paper, and refrigerate for at least an hour until firm.

Preheat the oven to 350°. With a sharp knife, cut the roll of dough into ¼-inch-thick rounds and place them an inch apart on the prepared baking sheet or sheets. Bake in the middle of the oven for about 10 minutes, or until the cookies are firm and light brown. After removing the cookies from the oven, let them cool for a few minutes on the baking sheet. With a spatula transfer them to a rack to cool completely. *Heidesand* cookies can be stored for several weeks in tightly sealed jars or tins.

NOTE: For more elaborate cookies, divide the dough in half after it has been mixed and work 1 tablespoon of unsweetened cocoa into one of the halves with your fingers. Then roll both halves out into similarly shaped rectangles about ⅛ inch thick and place one on top of the other. Roll the double thickness of dough jelly-roll fashion into a long cylinder, wrap it in wax paper and refrigerate. Then cut it into rounds as described above. The finished cookies will have a pattern of colored swirls.

Cakes and Desserts

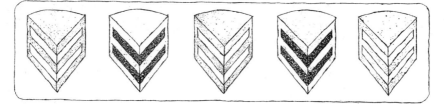

Königskuchen

LOAF CAKE WITH RAISINS, ALMONDS AND RUM

To make one 10-inch loaf cake

1 tablespoon butter, softened
¼ cup fine dry white bread crumbs
¾ cup seedless raisins
¾ cup dried currants
¼ cup dark rum
½ pound (2 sticks) unsalted butter, softened
1¼ cups sugar

7 egg yolks
1¾ cups all-purpose flour
1½ teaspoons double-acting baking powder
¾ cup blanched almonds, pulverized in an electric blender or with a nut grinder or mortar and pestle
1 teaspoon finely grated lemon peel
7 egg whites

Coat the bottom and sides of a 5-by-10-by-2½-inch loaf pan with 1 tablespoon of soft butter. Add the bread crumbs and tip the pan from side to side to spread the crumbs evenly on the buttered surfaces. Invert the pan and tap it gently on a table to remove any excess crumbs. Set aside. Combine the raisins and currants with the rum in a small bowl, and let them soak for at least 20 minutes. Preheat the oven to 350°.

In a large bowl, cream the unsalted butter and sugar together by mashing and beating them against the sides of the bowl with a large spoon until light and fluffy. Then beat in the egg yolks, one at a time, and continue beating for 10 minutes.

Combine the flour and the baking powder, and beat them into the sugar and egg mixture, ¼ cup at a time. When all the flour has been absorbed, stir in the raisins and currants with the rum, and the almonds and lemon peel. In a large bowl, beat the egg whites with a wire whisk or a rotary or electric beater until they form stiff peaks on the beater when it is lifted out of the bowl. Fold gently but thoroughly into the batter.

Pour the batter into the prepared loaf pan, smooth the top with a spatula, and bake in the middle of the oven for 1½ hours, or until the top is light brown and a cake tester inserted into the center of the cake comes out clean. Cool in the pan for 4 or 5 minutes, then run a sharp knife around the inside edges of the pan and turn it out on a rack to cool completely.

Frankfurter Kranz
LAYER CAKE WITH BUTTER-CREAM FILLING AND PRALINE TOPPING

Frankfurter Kranz is a frankly extravagant cake that uses more than a dozen eggs, almost a pound and a half of butter, and over a cup of rum. Even in Germany, it is a special treat served only on the most elegant occasions.

To serve 10

THE CAKE
1 tablespoon butter, softened
2 tablespoons flour
¼ pound plus 4 tablespoons
    unsalted butter (1½ sticks),
    softened
1 cup sugar

1 cup all-purpose flour
1½ teaspoons finely grated lemon
    peel
6 eggs, at room temperature
¾ cup cornstarch
1 tablespoon double-acting baking
    powder
¾ cup rum

Preheat the oven to 325°. With a pastry brush or paper towel, coat the bottom, sides and tube of a 9-inch tube cake pan with 1 tablespoon of soft butter. Sprinkle the butter with 2 tablespoons of flour, tip the pan from side to side to spread the flour evenly, then invert it and rap the bottom sharply to remove the excess flour.

In a large bowl, cream ¼ pound plus 4 tablespoons of butter, 1 cup of sugar, 1 tablespoon of the flour and the lemon peel together by mashing and beating them against the sides of the bowl with a large spoon. Then beat in the eggs, one at a time, and continue to beat until smooth. Combine the remaining flour, cornstarch and baking powder, and sift them into the butter a little at a time, beating well after each addition.

Pour the batter into the cake pan and bake in the middle of the oven for 40 minutes, or until a cake tester inserted in the center comes out clean. Let the cake cool in the pan for 10 minutes. Then run a knife around the inside edges of the pan, place a wire cake rack on top and, grasping rack and pan firmly together, turn them over. The cake should slide easily out of the pan. When the cake has cooled completely, slice it crosswise with a large, sharp knife into three equal layers. (It is easiest to cut if baked a day in advance.) Spread the layers on a long strip of foil or wax paper and sprinkle each layer with ¼ cup of rum.

FILLING
10 egg yolks, at room temperature
1 pound unsalted butter (4 sticks),
    softened

1⅓ cups sugar
⅛ teaspoon cream of tartar
⅔ cup water
½ cup rum

To make the butter-cream filling, beat the 10 egg yolks in a large bowl with a whisk or a rotary or electric beater until they are thick and lemon colored. Set the beaten yolks aside. Cream the pound of soft butter by mashing and beating it against the sides of a bowl with a large spoon until it is light and fluffy. Set it aside.

Bring 1⅓ cups of sugar, ⅛ teaspoon cream of tartar and ⅔ cup of water to a boil over moderate heat in a small saucepan, stirring only until the sugar dissolves. Increase the heat to high and boil the syrup briskly without stirring until it reaches a temperature of 236° on a candy thermometer, or until a drop spooned into cold water immediately forms a soft ball.

Pour the syrup in a thin stream into the reserved egg yolks, beating constantly with a whisk or a rotary or electric beater. Continue beating for 4 or 5 minutes longer, or until the mixture is thick and smooth. Gradually add ½ cup of rum, and continue to beat until the mixture has cooled to room temperature and is thick. Now beat in the reserved butter, a tablespoon or so at a time, and when it is completely absorbed, cover the bowl with wax paper or plastic wrap and refrigerate the butter cream for at least 30 minutes, or until it can be spread easily.

TOPPING

1 tablespoon butter	½ cup cold water
1 cup sugar	1 cup blanched almonds

Meanwhile prepare the praline topping in the following fashion: With a pastry brush or paper towel, coat a baking sheet with 1 tablespoon of butter and set it aside. In a small saucepan, bring 1 cup of sugar and ½ cup of water to a boil over moderate heat, stirring until the sugar dissolves. Increase the heat to high and boil briskly, undisturbed, until the syrup reaches a temperature of 236° on a candy thermometer, or a drop of syrup spooned into cold water immediately forms a soft ball. Stir in the nuts and cook until the syrup reaches a temperature of 310° on a candy thermometer, or until the syrup caramelizes and turns a rich golden brown.

Pour the syrup evenly onto the baking sheet. When it is cool and firm, break the praline into small pieces and pulverize it in a blender for a few seconds or crush it with a mortar and pestle. Spread it out on wax paper.

To assemble the cake, place the bottom layer in the center of a large cake plate and, with a spatula, spread it with about ½ inch of butter cream. Set the second layer on top and spread it with another ½-inch layer of butter cream. Finally set the top layer of cake in place and mask the top and sides with the remaining butter cream (if you like, reserve some butter cream to decorate the cake). Gently press the crushed praline over the sides of the cake and sprinkle the remainder over the top. Any extra butter cream may be piped on top of the cake through a pastry tube fitted with a decorative tip.

Schwarzwälder Kirschtorte
BLACK FOREST CHERRY CAKE

To serve 8 to 10

CHOCOLATE CURLS
8 ounces semisweet bar chocolate

To make chocolate curls to garnish the cake, the bar or chunks of chocolate should be at room temperature but not soft. Hold the chocolate over wax paper or foil and shave the bar or square into thin curls with a sharp narrow-bladed vegetable peeler. Draw the peeler along the wide surface of the chocolate for large curls, and along the narrow side for small ones. Handle the chocolate as little as possible. Refrigerate or freeze the curls until you are ready to use them.

CAKE

1 tablespoon butter, softened	1 teaspoon vanilla extract
6 tablespoons flour	1 cup sugar
10 tablespoons sweet butter	½ cup sifted flour
6 eggs, at room temperature	½ cup unsweetened cocoa

Preheat the oven to 350°. With a pastry brush or paper towel, lightly coat the bottoms and sides of three 7-inch round cake pans with soft butter using about 1 tablespoon of butter in all. Sprinkle 2 tablespoons of flour into each pan, tip them from side to side to spread the flour evenly, then invert the pans and rap them sharply on a table to remove any excess flour. Set the pans aside.

Clarify 10 tablespoons of butter in a small saucepan by melting it slowly over low heat without letting it brown. Let it rest for a minute off the heat, then skim off the foam. Spoon the clear butter into a bowl and set aside. Discard the milky solids at the bottom of the pan.

In an electric mixer, beat the eggs, vanilla and 1 cup of sugar together at high speed for at least 10 minutes, or until the mixture is thick and fluffy and has almost tripled in bulk. (By hand with a rotary beater, this may take as long as 20 minutes of uninterrupted beating.)

Combine the ½ cup of sifted flour and the unsweetened cocoa in a sifter. A little at a time sift the mixture over the eggs, folding it in gently with a rubber spatula. Finally, add the clarified butter 2 tablespoons at a time. Do not overmix. Gently pour the batter into the prepared cake pans dividing it evenly among the three of them.

Bake in the middle of the oven for 10 to 15 minutes, or until a cake tester inserted into the center of each cake comes out clean. Remove the cakes from the oven and let them cool in the pans for about 5 minutes. Then run a sharp knife around the edge of each cake and turn them out on racks to cool completely.

SYRUP   1 cup cold water
¾ cup sugar   ⅓ cup kirsch

Meanwhile, prepare the kirsch syrup in the following fashion: Combine ¾ cup of sugar and 1 cup of cold water in a small saucepan and bring to a boil over moderate heat, stirring only until the sugar dissolves. Boil briskly, uncovered, for 5 minutes, then remove the pan from the heat and when the syrup has cooled to lukewarm stir in the kirsch.

Transfer the cakes to a long strip of wax paper and prick each layer lightly in several places with the tines of a long fork. Sprinkle the layers evenly with the syrup and let them rest for at least 5 minutes.

FILLING AND TOPPING   cherries or 1 cup drained and
3 cups chilled heavy cream   rinsed canned sour red cherries
½ cup confectioners' sugar   Fresh sweet red cherries with stems,
¼ cup kirsch   or substitute maraschino cherries
1 cup poached pitted fresh red   with stems, drained and rinsed

If you are using fresh cherries for the filling, poach them in the following fashion: Remove their stems and pits, then combine them with 2 cups of water and ¾ cup of sugar in a small saucepan. Bring to a boil over high heat, then reduce the heat to low, simmer for 5 minutes, or until the cherries are tender. Drain them in a colander, discarding the syrup, and pat the cherries completely dry with paper towels. Canned cherries need only be rinsed in cold water and patted completely dry with paper towels.

In a large chilled bowl, beat the cream with a whisk or a rotary or electric beater until it thickens lightly. Then sift ½ cup of confectioners' sugar over the cream and continue beating until the cream forms firm peaks on the beater when it is lifted out of the bowl. Pour in the ¼ cup kirsch in a thin stream, and beat only until the kirsch is absorbed.

To assemble the cake, place one of the three layers in the center of a serving plate. With a spatula, spread the top with a ½-inch-thick layer of whipped cream and strew the cup of fresh or canned cherries over it leaving about ½ inch of cream free of cherries around the perimeter. Gently set a second layer on top of the cherries and spread it with ½ inch of whipped cream. Then set the third layer in place. Spread the top and sides of the cake with the remaining cream.

With your fingers, gently press chocolate curls into the cream on the sides of the cake and arrange a few chocolate curls and fresh or maraschino cherries attractively on top.

Obsttorte
MIXED FRUIT TART

To serve 8 to 10

PASTRY
2 cups all-purpose flour
¼ cup sugar
2 egg yolks

1 hard-cooked egg yolk, forced
  through a fine sieve
½ pound (2 sticks) unsalted butter,
  melted and cooled

Sift the flour and sugar into a large bowl and make a well in the center. Drop in the raw egg yolks and the sieved, cooked yolk. Mix them together with your fingertips or a large spoon. When the ingredients are well combined, mix in the melted butter a few tablespoons at a time, and continue to mix until the dough is smooth and pliable. On a lightly floured surface pat and shape the dough into a roll about 6 inches long and 2½ inches in diameter, wrap it in wax paper and refrigerate for at least 30 minutes.

Preheat the oven to 325°. With a sharp knife, carefully slice the pastry roll into rounds about ¼ inch thick. Arrange the rounds in a single layer in a 9-inch springform cake pan. With your fingers, gently pat the rounds and smooth the edges so that they completely cover the bottom of the pan and no empty spaces show between them. Stand the remaining slices around the sides of the pan, pressing them down about ½ inch into the bottom layer to secure them to the base and to create a scalloped effect around the top. Refrigerate for 10 minutes, then prick the surface of the dough all over with the tines of a fork without penetrating through to the bottom of the pan. Bake in the middle of the oven for 40 minutes, or until the pastry is firm and light brown. Transfer the pastry shell to a cake rack and let it cool completely before removing the sides of the pan.

FILLING
1 envelope unflavored gelatin
1¼ cups canned fruit juice,
  preferably a mixture of juices
  drained from canned fruit
5 to 6 cups combined fresh and

drained, canned fruit such as
strawberries, raspberries, orange
sections, apple wedges, canned
peach halves or slices, pitted green
plums, pear halves, pitted apricots,
pineapple slices

In a heatproof measuring cup or small bowl, sprinkle the gelatin over the fruit juice. When the gelatin has softened for 2 or 3 minutes, set the cup in a small skillet of simmering water and cook over low heat, stirring constantly, until the gelatin dissolves completely. Remove the cup from the skillet and let the gelatin cool slightly.

With a pastry brush, lightly coat the bottom of the pastry shell with the gelatin to seal it and let it set for about 5 minutes. Then with paper towels, pat the pieces of fruit you plan to use completely dry. Arrange the fruit on the gelatin, in decorative concentric circles, overlapping the pieces slightly to cover the bottom of the shell completely and filling the shell to within about ¼ inch of the top. The number of layers you will need depends on the size and shape of the fruit.

Glaze the final layer with a thin coating of gelatin. If the gelatin becomes too thick to brush smoothly over the fruit, return it to the warm water for several minutes. Set the tart aside.

ALMOND COATING

| 1½ cups thinly sliced blanched almonds | 1 egg white |
| | 1 tablespoon superfine sugar |

Preheat the oven to 350°. Spread the almonds in a shallow baking pan and bake or toast, turning them frequently, for 5 minutes, or until they are light brown. With a wire whisk or a rotary or electric beater, beat the egg white until it thickens slightly. Sprinkle the sugar over it and beat until the white forms firm peaks on the beater when it is lifted out of the bowl.

With a small metal spatula coat the outside of the pastry shell evenly with the meringue and press the almond slices against it to secure them. The entire outer surface should finally be covered with almonds.

TOPPING

| 1 cup chilled heavy cream | 1 tablespoon confectioners' sugar |
| | A few drops of vanilla extract |

Beat the cream with a whisk or a rotary or electric beater until it thickens slightly, then sprinkle with confectioners' sugar and vanilla, and continue beating until the mixture forms stiff peaks on the beater when it is lifted out of the bowl. Transfer the whipped cream to a bowl and serve it separately with the tart.

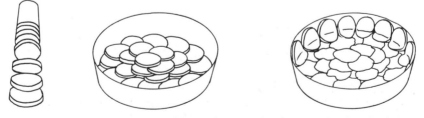

To make the mixed fruit tart pastry shell (*recipe opposite*), shape the dough into a 2½-inch roll, chill, then cut it into ¼-inch slices (*left*). Fit one layer of the slices into a 9-inch springform pan, overlapping them slightly, and press the slices gently together to cover the bottom (*center*). Stand the remaining pastry slices around the edge of the pan, pressing them firmly into the corners (*right*).

101

Mandeltorte

ALMOND LAYER CAKE

To serve 6 to 8

	2 whole eggs
CAKE	6 egg yolks
1 ½ cups blanched almonds	½ cup sugar
2 tablespoons butter, softened	⅓ cup flour
4 tablespoons fine dry bread crumbs	6 egg whites

Preheat the oven to 350°. Spread the almonds in a shallow roasting pan or jelly-roll pan and toast them in the oven, turning them occasionally, for about 5 minutes, or until they are golden brown. Pulverize the nuts in an electric blender or with a nut grinder or a mortar and pestle, and set them aside. With a pastry brush or paper towel, lightly coat the bottom and sides of two round 8-inch layer-cake pans with 1 tablespoon of soft butter each. Sprinkle 2 tablespoons of bread crumbs into each pan, tip the pans from side to side to spread the crumbs evenly, then invert the pans, and rap them gently on a table to remove the excess crumbs. Set the pans aside.

With an electric mixer, a whisk or rotary beater, beat the eggs, egg yolks and sugar together until the mixture is thick enough to fall back on itself in a slowly dissolving ribbon when the beater is lifted from the bowl. Then beat in the flour and ground almonds.

In a separate bowl, beat the egg whites with a whisk, rotary or electric beater until they form firm unwavering peaks on the beater when it is lifted from the bowl. With a rubber spatula, gently but thoroughly fold the egg whites into the egg yolk batter using an over-under cutting motion rather than a stirring motion. Pour the batter into the cake pans and spread it out evenly. Bake in the middle of the oven for 20 minutes, or until a cake tester inserted in the center comes out clean. Cool the cakes in the pans for 5 minutes, then run a sharp knife around the outside edges of the cakes, and turn them out on a rack. Cool completely.

GLAZE AND FILLING	2 tablespoons rum
2¼ cups sifted confectioners' sugar	1 tablespoon fresh lemon juice
1 egg white	½ cup raspberry or strawberry jam

Meanwhile, combine the confectioners' sugar, egg white, rum and lemon juice in a large bowl. Beat these ingredients together with a whisk or a rotary beater for about 5 minutes, or until they are smooth and as thick as heavy cream. If the glaze seems too thin, beat in additional confectioners' sugar, a teaspoonful at a time.

To assemble, place one of the layers in the center of a large serving platter. With a small metal spatula or a knife, spread raspberry or strawberry jam over the cake. Set the other layer on top, and coat it with the rum glaze.

Griesstorte

FARINA LAYER CAKE WITH ALMONDS

To serve 6

2 tablespoons butter, softened

2 tablespoons fine dry white bread crumbs

6 egg yolks

¾ cup sugar

1 teaspoon finely grated lemon peel

1 tablespoon fresh lemon juice

1 cup regular farina (not the quick-cooking type)

½ cup blanched almonds pulverized in an electric blender or a nut grinder or mortar and pestle

6 egg whites

Apricot jam

Rum glaze *(see Mandeltorte, opposite)*

Coat the bottom and sides of an 8-inch springform cake pan with the soft butter. Pour in the bread crumbs and tip the pan from side to side to spread the crumbs as evenly as possible. Then invert the pan and tap it gently to remove any excess crumbs. Set aside. Preheat the oven to 350°.

In an electric mixer beat the egg yolks, sugar, lemon peel and lemon juice together at high speed for about 5 minutes, or until they are thick and lemon colored. Then add the farina and beat at medium speed for another 10 minutes, or until the batter is thick enough to fall back on itself in a ribbon when the beater is lifted from the bowl. (To make the batter by hand with a whisk or a rotary beater, follow the same procedure but increase the total beating time to about 20 minutes.)

Stir in the pulverized almonds. In a separate bowl, beat the egg whites with a wire whisk or a rotary or electric beater until they form stiff peaks on the beater when it is lifted out of the bowl. With a rubber spatula, fold the egg whites gently but thoroughly into the batter using an over-under cutting motion rather than a stirring motion.

Pour the batter into the springform pan, spread it out evenly and bake in the middle of the oven for 45 minutes, or until the top is lightly browned and a cake tester inserted into the center of the *Griesstorte* comes out clean. Cool the cake in the pan for 3 or 4 minutes, then turn it out onto a rack to cool completely.

With a long, sharp knife, carefully cut the cake into two layers, place the bottom layer on a serving plate and spread it generously with apricot jam. Gently set the second layer in place, and spread it evenly with a light coating of rum glaze.

Mohnstriezel

POPPY-SEED CAKE

To make two 10-inch loaves

DOUGH

¼ cup lukewarm water (110° to 115°)

3 packages active dry yeast

½ cup plus ½ teaspoon sugar

½ cup lukewarm milk (110° to 115°)

4 cups sifted all-purpose flour

2 eggs, at room temperature

¼ pound unsalted butter, cut into ¼-inch pieces and softened

Place the poppy seeds in a bowl, pour in enough boiling water to cover them by an inch and soak for 3 hours.

Pour the lukewarm water into a small, shallow bowl and sprinkle the yeast and ½ teaspoon of the sugar over it. Let the yeast and sugar stand 2 or 3 minutes, then stir to dissolve them completely. Set in a warm, draft-free spot, such as an unlighted oven, for 3 to 5 minutes, or until the mixture almost doubles in volume.

Transfer the yeast to a large mixing bowl. Dissolve the ½ cup of sugar in the milk and then stir the milk into the yeast. Beat in 3 cups of the sifted flour about ¼ cup at a time. Beat in the eggs one at a time and then the ¼ pound butter broken into bits, and continue to beat until the dough can be gathered into a compact ball. Transfer it to a lightly floured board and knead in the remaining cup of flour a few tablespoons at a time, pushing the dough down with the heels of your hands, pressing it forward and folding it back on itself. Knead until all the flour is incorporated and the dough is stiff and quite dry. Shape it into a rough ball, place it in a mixing bowl, and add enough cold water to cover the dough by several inches. In 10 to 15 minutes, the top of the ball of dough should rise above the surface of the water.

Remove the dough from the water and pat the surface as dry as you can with paper towels. Return it to a floured board, punch it down, and knead again for about 10 minutes, until the dough is smooth and elastic. Shape the dough into a ball, place it in a lightly buttered bowl, and cover loosely with a kitchen towel. Let the dough rise in a warm draft-free place for about 30 minutes, or until it doubles in bulk.

FILLING

½ pound poppy seeds

⅓ cup finely chopped blanched almonds

1 cup seedless raisins

2 teaspoons finely grated lemon peel

1 cup milk

1 cup sugar

2 tablespoons all-purpose flour

1 egg yolk

1 egg white

2 tablespoons soft butter plus 8 tablespoons melted butter

1 egg, lightly beaten with 1 tablespoon heavy cream

Meanwhile, for the filling, drain the poppy seeds and spread them out on paper towels to dry. Then pulverize them, ½ cup or so at a time, in an electric blender or with a mortar and pestle and combine them with the almonds, raisins and lemon peel in a large bowl.

In a heavy saucepan, combine ¾ cup of the milk and the sugar and bring to a boil over moderate heat. Reduce the heat to low. With a whisk, beat the 2 tablespoons of flour into the remaining ¼ cup of milk, then slowly beat it into the simmering milk. Again bring to a boil, whisking constantly, until the mixture is thick and smooth. Pour it over the poppy-seed mixture and stir well. Then beat in the egg yolk. In a separate bowl, beat the egg white until it forms firm unwavering peaks on the beater when it is lifted out of the bowl. With a rubber spatula, fold the egg white gently but thoroughly, into the poppy-seed filling.

Coat the bottom and sides of two 5-by-10-by-2 ½-inch loaf pans with 2 tablespoons of soft butter and set them aside. Preheat the oven to 375°. When the dough has risen, punch it down and divide it into two equal pieces. On a lightly floured surface, roll each half into a rectangle about 10 by 15 inches and a little less than ¼ inch thick. With a spatula, spread the filling evenly over the two rectangles to within ½ inch of their edges. Dribble 4 tablespoons of melted butter over each and then shape them as follows: First roll one long side to the center, jelly-roll fashion, then roll the opposite side to the center jelly-roll fashion. Firmly holding both sides together, turn each cake over so that the seam is on the bottom when the cake is set in its pan. Brush the tops with the egg and cream mixture and bake in the middle of the oven for 1 hour, or until the cakes are golden brown and crusty. Cool in the pans for 5 minutes or so, then turn them out on a cake rack. Cool completely before serving.

To shape each poppy-seed cake *(recipe above)*, roll half of the dough into a 10-by-15-inch rectangle and spread it evenly with half of the poppy-seed filling *(above left)*. With your hands, gently roll up both sides, jelly-roll fashion, to meet in the middle of the cake *(center)*. Holding the cake firmly, carefully turn it over *(right)* and set it seam side down in a buttered loaf pan, ready to be baked.

Streuselkuchen

SUGAR-CRUMB CAKE

To make one 11-by-17-inch cake

CAKE

¼ cup lukewarm water (110° to 115°)
1 package active dry yeast
¼ teaspoon plus ⅓ cup sugar
¾ cup lukewarm milk (110° to 115°)

1 teaspoon finely grated lemon peel
1 egg, at room temperature
2 egg yolks, at room temperature
3 cups sifted all-purpose flour
7 tablespoons unsalted butter, softened

Pour the lukewarm water into a small shallow mixing bowl and sprinkle it with the yeast and ¼ teaspoon of the sugar. Let the mixture stand for 2 or 3 minutes, then stir to dissolve the yeast completely. Set the bowl aside in a warm, draft-free place—such as a turned-off oven—for about 5 minutes, or until the mixture almost doubles in volume. Then stir in the lukewarm milk and the lemon peel.

In a large mixing bowl, beat the remaining ⅓ cup of sugar, the egg and the egg yolks together, and then stir in the yeast and milk mixture. Add the 3 cups of sifted flour, a cup or so at a time, beating well after each addition. Continue to beat until a soft dough is formed. Then beat in 6 tablespoons of the softened butter, 1 tablespoon at a time, and gather the dough into a compact ball.

Place the dough on a lightly floured surface and knead it by pushing it down with the heels of your hands, pressing it forward and folding it back on itself. Repeat this process for about 10 minutes, or until the dough is smooth and elastic. Gather it into a ball again, place it in a buttered bowl and dust the top lightly with flour. Cover the bowl with a towel and put it aside in a warm draft-free place for about 40 minutes, or until the dough doubles in bulk.

Preheat the oven to 375°. With a pastry brush, lightly coat the bottom and sides of an 11-by-17-inch jelly-roll pan with the remaining 1 tablespoon of soft butter. Set aside.

TOPPING

½ pound butter (2 sticks), cut into
  bits and thoroughly chilled
2 cups all-purpose flour

⅔ cup sugar
1 teaspoon ground cinnamon
¼ cup melted butter

Prepare the *Streusel* topping by combining the ½ pound of chilled butter bits, 2 cups of flour, ⅔ cup sugar, and 1 teaspoon of cinnamon in a large bowl. Working quickly, rub the flour and fat together with your fingertips until they look like flakes of coarse meal.

When the dough has risen, punch it down and knead it on a lightly floured surface for 3 or 4 minutes. Then place it in the jelly-roll pan and stretch and smooth it out with your hands or a rolling pin until it covers the bottom of the pan.

Strew the *Streusel* mixture evenly over the top of the cake and sprinkle it with ¼ cup of melted butter. Bake in the middle of the oven for 45 minutes, or until the top is crusty. To serve, cut the cake into 2-inch squares and serve warm or at room temperature. Traditionally, *Streuselkuchen* is served at the German coffee table.

NOTE: To make *Pflaumenkuchen* or plum cake, prepare the dough as described above, but in place of the *Streusel,* cover the top with neat rows of firm ripe purple freestone plums, about 3 pounds.

Cut the plums almost in half, pit and spread them open. Overlapping the plums slightly, stand them flesh side up in parallel rows across the entire width of the cake. Sprinkle them evenly with 1 cup of sugar mixed with 1 teaspoon of cinnamon, and before baking dribble ¼ cup of melted butter evenly over the top of the cake.

Apfelkuchen, or apple cake, may be made in the same fashion. Peel, core and slice 6 medium-sized cooking apples, and toss them with 2 tablespoons of lemon juice, 1 cup of sugar and 1 teaspoon of cinnamon.

Arrange the apple slices in parallel rows side by side across the width of the cake, and before baking dribble ¼ cup of melted butter over them.

Apfelkuchen

APPLE AND RUM CUSTARD CAKE

To serve 6 to 8

2 tablespoons melted butter

FILLING

¼ cup dried currants
¼ cup rum
½ cup fresh, white bread crumbs

6 medium-sized tart cooking apples
(about 2 pounds), peeled, cored
and cut into slices about ¼ inch
thick

Place the currants in a small bowl, pour the rum over them, and let them soak for at least 20 minutes. Preheat the oven to 350°.

PASTRY

2 cups all-purpose flour
¼ pound plus 4 tablespoons
unsalted butter, softened

4 egg yolks
2 tablespoons sugar
2 tablespoons finely grated lemon
peel

Meanwhile make the pastry. Combine the flour and ¼ pound plus 4 tablespoons of butter in a large bowl and, working quickly, use your fingertips to rub the flour and fat together until they look like flakes of coarse meal. With a large spoon, beat in 4 egg yolks, one at a time, then beat in 2 tablespoons of sugar and the lemon peel. With your fingers pat and press the pastry evenly into the bottom and sides of an 8-inch springform cake pan 2 inches high.

Now begin to fill the pastry shell in the following fashion: Stir the bread crumbs and 2 tablespoons of melted butter together in a small bowl, sprinkle the mixture evenly over the dough and spread the apples over it. Drain the currants and set the rum aside. Then scatter the currants over the apples. Bake in the middle of the oven for 10 minutes.

CUSTARD

2 whole eggs
2 egg yolks
⅓ cup sugar

1¾ cups heavy cream
2 tablespoons sugar combined with
2 tablespoons melted butter

During this first stage of baking, beat the 2 eggs, the 2 egg yolks and ⅓ cup of sugar with a wire whisk or a rotary or electric beater until they are thick and lemon colored. Beat in the reserved rum and the cream and pour half of it evenly over the apples in the partly baked cake. Bake the tart for 20 more minutes, or until the custard is set, then pour in the remaining liquid custard and bake for 30 minutes longer. Sprinkle the top of the tart with the 2 tablespoons of sugar mixed with the melted butter. Bake in the top third of the oven for 15 or 20 minutes, or until the top of the tart browns lightly.

Remove the pan from the oven and let the tart cool completely before removing the springform. With a wide spatula, slide the tart onto a cake plate and serve.

Apfelbettelmann
APPLE AND PUMPERNICKEL CRUMB DESSERT

To serve 4

9 tablespoons butter, softened
½ cup currants
5 tablespoons rum
1½ cups fine pumpernickel bread crumbs, made in the blender from fresh German-style dark

pumpernickel bread
½ cup coarsely chopped almonds or hazelnuts
¾ cup sugar
1 teaspoon finely grated lemon peel
1½ teaspoons ground cinnamon
4 medium-sized tart cooking apples

Preheat the oven to 350° and coat the inner surfaces of a 6- to 8-cup soufflé or baking dish with 2 tablespoons of the softened butter. Melt 5 tablespoons of the butter and set aside.

In a large mixing bowl, soak the currants in the rum for 30 minutes. Then add the bread crumbs, chopped nuts, ½ cup of the sugar, melted butter, lemon peel and cinnamon, and stir until all the ingredients are well combined. With a small, sharp knife, quarter, peel and core the apples, and cut them lengthwise into ¼-inch slices. Drop the slices into another bowl and sprinkle them with the remaining ¼ cup of sugar, turning the slices about with a wooden spoon to coat them evenly. With a spatula, spread about one third of the bread-crumb mixture on the bottom of the baking dish and strew about one half of the apple slices evenly over it. Repeat with another layer of the bread-crumb mixture and cover with the remaining apples. Spread the remaining bread-crumb mixture over the apples and dot the crumbs with the remaining 2 tablespoons of butter. Bake in the middle of the oven for 30 to 40 minutes, or until the apples are tender and show no resistance when pierced with the tip of a sharp knife. Serve at once directly from the baking dish. If you like you may sprinkle the top with cinnamon and sugar.

Schokoladenpudding
STEAMED CHOCOLATE PUDDING

To serve 8

2 tablespoons butter, softened
1⅓ cups plus 3 tablespoons sugar
2½ cups blanched almonds, coarsely
    chopped
½ pound semisweet chocolate, cut
    into small chunks
3 tablespoons strong coffee, made

from 1 teaspoon instant coffee and
    3 tablespoons boiling water
½ pound unsalted butter, softened
10 egg yolks
10 egg whites
2 cups heavy cream, chilled
3 tablespoons confectioners' sugar
⅛ teaspoon vanilla extract

With a pastry brush and 2 tablespoons of softened butter, coat the bottom and sides of a 2-quart steamed pudding mold, that is, a mold with a snugly fitting cover. Pour in 3 tablespoons of sugar, and tip the mold from side to side to spread the sugar evenly. Then turn the mold over and knock out the excess sugar. Set aside.

Preheat the oven to 350°. Spread the almonds out evenly in a shallow roasting pan. Toast them in the middle of the oven for about 10 minutes, stirring them occasionally until they are light brown. Be careful not to let them burn. Set them aside in a bowl.

Melt the chocolate with the coffee, stirring constantly, in a heavy 1-quart saucepan over low heat or in a double boiler placed over simmering water. Then cool to lukewarm.

In a large mixing bowl, beat the ½ pound of butter and 1⅓ cups of sugar together, with a large spoon, mashing and beating against the side of the bowl until the mixture is light and fluffy. Beat in the egg yolks, one at a time, then little by little add the melted chocolate and coffee, and continue to beat until the batter is smooth. Stir in the almonds.

In a separate bowl, with a wire whisk or a rotary or electric beater, beat the egg whites until they form soft peaks on the beater when it is lifted out of the bowl. Stir about one quarter of the whites into the chocolate mixture to lighten it, then pour it over the remaining egg whites and gently but thoroughly fold them together. Spoon the pudding into the prepared mold, smooth the top with a spatula and cover the mold tightly.

Place the mold in a large pot and add enough water to come two thirds of the way up the side of the mold. Bring the water to a boil over high heat, reduce the heat to its lowest point, cover the pot and simmer undisturbed for 1 hour. Then remove the mold from the water and wipe it dry. Remove the cover and unmold the pudding in the following fashion: Run a long, sharp knife around the inside edges of the mold, then place a heated serving plate over the mold. Grasping mold and plate together turn them over. Rap the plate on a table and the pudding should slide out easily.

With a wire whisk or a rotary or electric beater, whip the chilled cream in a large chilled bowl until it thickens slightly. Sprinkle the cream with the confectioners' sugar and vanilla and continue to beat until the cream is stiff.

Serve the pudding while it is still hot, accompanied by the whipped cream presented separately in a bowl.

Haselnusscreme
HAZELNUT CREAM PUDDING

To serve 4

2 teaspoons unflavored gelatin
2 tablespoons cold water
1 cup shelled and blanched hazelnuts, pulverized in a blender or with a

nut grinder or mortar and pestle
1¼ cups milk
3 egg yolks
½ cup sugar
1 teaspoon vanilla extract
1 cup heavy cream

In a heatproof measuring cup, sprinkle the gelatin over the cold water. When the gelatin has softened for 2 or 3 minutes, set the cup in a small skillet of simmering water and cook over low heat, stirring constantly, until the gelatin dissolves completely. Remove the skillet from the heat, but leave the cup of gelatin in the water to keep warm.

Combine the nuts and milk in a heavy 2- to 3-quart saucepan and heat, stirring constantly, until bubbles form around the edge of the pan. Remove from the heat. With a whisk or a rotary or electric beater, beat the egg yolks and sugar together in a mixing bowl for 3 or 4 minutes, or until the yolks are pale yellow and thick. Beating constantly, pour the hot milk in a thin stream over the yolks, then pour this custard mixture into the saucepan. Cook over low heat, stirring constantly, until it thickens enough to coat a spoon heavily. Do not let the custard come to a boil or it may curdle.

Remove the pan from the heat and stir in the dissolved gelatin and the vanilla extract. Transfer the custard to a mixing bowl, preferably stainless steel, and set it aside and let it cool to room temperature. With a whisk or a rotary or electric beater, beat the cream in a large chilled bowl until it holds soft peaks. Set the bowl of custard into a pot or another larger bowl filled with crushed ice, and stir the custard with a metal spoon until it is cold but not set. Beat thoroughly with a wire whisk if any lumps form. Immediately pour the whipped cream over the custard and with a rubber spatula fold them together gently but thoroughly. Spoon the mixture into a 1-quart serving bowl or four individual 8-ounce dessert dishes, cover tightly with foil or plastic wrap, and refrigerate for at least 3 hours, or until firm.

NOTE: If you cannot buy blanched hazelnuts, drop shelled nuts into a pan of water and boil them briskly for 2 minutes. Drain the hazelnuts in a sieve, and with a small, sharp knife peel them while they are still hot.

111

Apfelpfannkuchen
APPLE-FILLED PANCAKES

To make about 6 pancakes

FILLING
6 tablespoons butter
3 pounds tart cooking apples, peeled, cored and sliced into ¼-inch-thick wedges
2 tablespoons sugar mixed with 1 teaspoon ground cinnamon

In a heavy 12-inch skillet, melt 6 tablespoons of butter over moderate heat. When the foam subsides, drop in the apple slices and sprinkle them with the mixed sugar and cinnamon. Cook, stirring gently from time to time, until the apples soften slightly and begin to color. Don't overcook. Set the skillet aside, off the heat.

PANCAKES
8 eggs
2½ cups milk
1 cup flour
4 teaspoons sugar
½ teaspoon salt
6 tablespoons butter
Confectioners' sugar

Preheat the broiler to its highest point. To make the pancake batter, combine the eggs and milk in a large mixing bowl and beat them with a whisk or fork only long enough to blend them. Do not overbeat. Mix the flour with 4 teaspoons of sugar and ½ teaspoon of salt and add it to the eggs and milk a few tablespoonfuls at a time, stirring constantly all the while.

In a heavy 10-inch skillet, melt 1 tablespoon of butter over moderate heat. When the foam subsides, pour in ½ cup of the batter and tip the pan from side to side so that the batter quickly covers the bottom. Strew ¾ cup of apples evenly over the batter and let the pancake cook for 3 minutes. Watch carefully for any sign of burning and regulate the heat accordingly. Pour a second ½ cup of batter over the apples and slide the skillet under the broiler 6 or 7 inches from the heat. Cook the pancake for 2 or 3 more minutes, or until the top is golden brown and firm to the touch. Watch carefully for any sign of burning.

Loosen the sides and bottom of the pancake with a metal spatula and slide the pancake onto a heated individual serving plate. The pancakes are best served at once but they may be covered with foil to keep them warm until they are all ready to be served. Add 1 tablespoon of additional butter to the skillet for each successive pancake. Just before serving, sprinkle the pancakes lightly with confectioners' sugar.

NOTE: Traditionally *Apfelpfannkuchen* are cooked entirely on top of the stove—a delicate process that involves turning the filled pancake without dislodging the apple filling. Finishing the pancake under the broiler is easier and safer for most cooks—and produces almost the same result.

Zitronencreme

LEMON-CREAM DESSERT

To serve 6

1 envelope unflavored gelatin
¼ cup cold water
3 egg yolks
½ cup plus 3 tablespoons sugar
¼ cup fresh lemon juice
2 teaspoons finely grated lemon peel

1 cup heavy cream
3 egg whites
1 lemon, cut lengthwise into halves
   and cut crosswise into paper-thin
   slices (optional)
½ cup heavy cream (optional)
1 teaspoon confectioners' sugar
  (optional)

In a heatproof measuring cup or small bowl, sprinkle the gelatin over ¼ cup of cold water. When the gelatin has softened for 2 or 3 minutes, set the cup in a small skillet of simmering water and stir until the gelatin dissolves completely. Remove the skillet from the heat, but leave the cup of gelatin in the skillet.

With a wire whisk or a rotary or electric beater, beat the egg yolks with ½ cup of the sugar until the yolks are pale yellow and thick enough to fall back in a ribbon when the beater is lifted from the bowl. Stir in the dissolved gelatin, the lemon juice and the lemon peel. With the same whisk or beater whip the cream in a large chilled bowl until it is firm enough to hold its shape softly. Then, with a rubber spatula, gently but thoroughly fold the cream into the egg and lemon mixture, using an over-under cutting motion rather than a stirring motion.

Wash and dry the whisk or beater; then, in a separate bowl, use it to beat the egg whites until they are frothy. Sprinkle in the remaining 3 tablespoons of sugar and continue beating until the egg whites are stiff enough to stand in unwavering peaks when the whisk is lifted from the bowl. Gently fold the egg whites into the lemon mixture and continue to fold until no trace of white can be seen in the mixture.

Spoon the lemon cream into six individual dessert dishes or into a large serving bowl. Cover it tightly and refrigerate it for at least 3 hours before serving.

If you like, you may garnish the dessert with lemon slices and whipped cream. Whip the cream with a wire whisk or a rotary or electric beater until it holds its shape softly, sprinkle it with confectioners' sugar, and beat until the cream is stiff enough to form firm, unwavering peaks. With a pastry bag fitted with a decorative tip, pipe rosettes or decorative swirls of whipped cream on top of the dessert.

Rauhreif
"FIRST FROST" APPLE AND CREAM DESSERT

To serve 4 to 6

1 cup heavy cream, chilled
6 tablespoons sugar
¼ teaspoon vanilla extract

⅓ cup fresh orange juice
2 tablespoons fresh lemon juice
6 large eating apples (preferably
    Rome Beauty or red or yellow
    Delicious), about 2 ½ pounds

In a large chilled mixing bowl, beat the cream with a whisk or a rotary or electric beater until it begins to thicken. Sprinkle in 3 tablespoons of sugar and the vanilla extract; continue beating until the cream is firm enough to hold stiff unwavering peaks on the beater when it is lifted from the bowl.

Combine the orange juice, lemon juice and the remaining 3 tablespoons of sugar in another large bowl. Working with one apple at a time, quarter, peel, and core it and immediately grate it into the sugared juice with the coarse side of a grater. Stir the grated apples occasionally to keep them well moistened and to prevent them from discoloring. Chill the whipped cream and the apple mixture separately until you are ready to serve them. (Tightly covered, whipped cream can be kept for an hour or so.) At the last possible minute, fold the apple mixture into the whipped cream with a rubber spatula, blending them together lightly but thoroughly. Spoon the apple cream into chilled individual dessert bowls or parfait glasses and serve immediately.

Weingelee
WINE JELLY WITH FRUIT

To serve 4 to 6

2 envelopes unflavored gelatin
1½ cups water
2 cups dry white wine
2 tablespoons fresh lemon juice
½ cup sugar
2 cups assorted fresh, canned or

thoroughly defrosted frozen fruit
such as peach halves or slices;
pitted apricots or apricot halves;
pear halves; pitted cherries, whole
strawberries or strawberry halves;
whole grapes or grape halves;
pineapple wedges, banana slices
or orange sections

In a small heatproof bowl, sprinkle the gelatin over 1 cup of the water. When the gelatin has softened for 2 or 3 minutes, set the bowl in a skillet of simmering water and cook over low heat, stirring constantly, until the gelatin dissolves. Remove the skillet from the heat, but leave the bowl of gelatin in the water. In a large bowl combine the wine, the remaining ½ cup of water, the lemon juice and sugar, and stir until the sugar dissolves. Thoroughly stir in the warm gelatin. Pour a ¼-inch layer of the mixture into a 5-cup mold, pack the mold into a bowl half filled with crushed ice or coarsely crushed ice cubes and refrigerate until firm. (Keep the remaining gelatin at room temperature so that it remains liquid and ready to use.)

Drain the fruit and spread the pieces between paper towels to dry them. Arrange a layer of various kinds of fruit on the surface of the set gelatin. Gradually pour over it enough liquid gelatin to reach almost but not quite to the top of the fruit. Chill again until set, then pour in enough gelatin to cover the fruit by ¼ inch. Chill. Repeat this process 4 or 5 more times, filling the mold with alternating layers of fruit and gelatin and refrigerating the mold after each step. Finally add enough gelatin to come to within ¼ inch of the top. Refrigerate for at least 6 hours, or until firm. (Any remaining gelatin may be chilled in a flat pan at the same time and used chopped or cut into decorative shapes as a garnish for the *Weingelee*.)

To unmold and serve, run a knife around the sides of the mold and dip the bottom in hot water for a few seconds. Wipe the mold dry, place a serving plate upside down over it, and, grasping plate and mold together, turn them over. Rap them on a table and the jelly should slide out easily. Chill until ready to serve. If you like, you may accompany *Weingelee* with whipped cream.

Backobstkompott
DRIED FRUIT COMPOTE

To serve 6 to 8

1½ pounds mixed dried fruits (about 5 cups)

2 cups sugar
A 2-inch length of cinnamon stick
Peel of 1 lemon, cut into ½-by-2-inch strips

Soak the fruit overnight, or for at least 12 hours in enough cold water to cover it by 1 inch. Drain the fruit in a colander. Measure the soaking liquid and if necessary add enough water to make 1 quart. Then pour it into a heavy 3- to 4-quart saucepan, add the sugar, cinnamon stick and lemon peel, and bring to a boil over moderate heat, stirring until the sugar dissolves. Drop in the drained fruit, reduce the heat to low and simmer, uncovered, stirring occasionally, for about 10 minutes, or until the fruit is tender and can be easily pierced with the tip of a fork. With a slotted spoon, transfer the fruit to a heatproof bowl. Then boil the syrup briskly over high heat for 5 minutes, or until it thickens slightly. Remove the pan from the heat and pour the syrup over the fruit. Serve the compote while it is still warm, or refrigerate until chilled. In Germany, *Backobstkompott* is usually served as an accompaniment to dumplings or meats. If you like, you may add ¼ cup of kirsch, brandy, rum or white wine to the fruit along with the syrup.

Recipe Index: English

Soups

Chicken giblet and barley soup.. 2
Cream of cauliflower soup 6
Hot beer soup 4
Lentil soup 3
Potato soup with cucumber... 5
Vegetable-beef soup with tiny dumplings............................. 4

Fish

Fillet of walleyed pike with mustard butter 7
"Fish for a hangover" with tomato sauce and pickles 11
Halibut under a mountain of cream.................................... 10
Rollmops.. 9
Walleyed pike baked in white wine 8

Meat and Poultry

Beef in spiced sour-cream sauce 18
Beef short ribs with spiced lemon-and-caper sauce 12
Beefsteak Tartar... 17
Berlin-style chicken fricassee.. 40
Boiled beef with chive sauce 15
Braised lamb shoulder with mustard and red wine sauce................ 26
Braised stuffed beef rolls.. 13
Braised stuffed veal roll... 22
Bratwurst in sweet-sour sauce 34
Calf's liver with apples and onion rings 38
Corned beef hash with salt herring................................... 37
Fresh ham, mock-boar style.. 32
Ham braised in burgundy... 33
Lamb chops in onion sauce 25
Marinated pot roast in sweet-and-sour sauce 16
Mixed meat and vegetable casserole 36
Poached meatballs in lemon-and-caper sauce 14
Pork chops in aspic.. 28
Pork chops with knockwurst and potatoes 30
Roast duck with apple and bread stuffing 43
Roast goose with apple, raisin and nut stuffing 38
Roasted smoked pork loin 31
Spareribs with pickle sauce 35
Steamed bratwurst in sour-cream sauce 34
Veal roast stuffed with kidney....................................... 24
Veal shanks in pickle sauce 19
Veal tongue, sweetbreads and mushrooms in white wine sauce 20

Game

Braised rabbit in spiced red wine sauce............................... 44
Game birds in burgundy.. 51
Pheasant in red wine... 52
Pheasant with giblet and crouton stuffing 53
Roast partridges with grapes 50
Roast saddle of venison with red wine sauce........................... 47
Venison cutlets with mushrooms...................................... 45
Venison tenderloin in spiced brandy sauce 49

Dumplings

Dessert dumplings with vanilla sauce................................. 58
Farina dumplings 59
Potato dessert dumplings with prune-butter filling 57
Potato dumplings.. 56
Tiny dumplings.. 55

Yeast dumplings 60

Vegetables

Baked kale with potatoes 66
Beans with fruit and vegetables. 72
Brussels sprouts with ham and tomatoes 70
Eggs with bacon, onions and potatoes 67
Endive baked with ham and cheese 68
Green herb sauce 73
Mushrooms with tomatoes and bacon 68
Pineapple sauerkraut 62
Potato pancakes with applesauce 65
Potatoes with apples 64
Red cabbage with apples. 63
Sauerkraut with wine and grapes 62
Sour potatoes 64
Steamed spiced sauerkraut 61
Stewed cucumbers with sour cream and dill 69
Yellow pea purée with bacon. 71

Salads

Celery root and apple salad. 77
Green bean salad 74
Hot potato salad with bacon 76
Leek salad 78
Pickled-beet salad. 75
Summer potato salad 76

Breads and Cookies

Almond crescent cookies 87
Brown butter cookies. 94
Chocolate pretzels. 84
Dresden Christmas fruit bread. 79
Gingerbread house. 90
Hazelnut macaroons 82
Honey cake. 88
Molded anise-seed cookies 86
Pressed hazelnut cookies 82
S-shaped butter cookies 83
Spice cookies 85
Spiced honey cookies. 89
White bread with caraway seeds 81

Cakes and Desserts

Almond layer cake 102
Apple and pumpernickel crumb dessert 109
Apple and rum custard cake. 108
Apple-filled pancakes. 112
Black Forest cherry cake 98
Dried fruit compote 115
Farina layer cake with almonds 103
"First frost" apple and cream dessert. 114
Hazelnut cream pudding 111
Layer cake with butter-cream filling and praline topping 96
Lemon cream dessert 113
Loaf cake with raisins, almonds and rum 95
Mixed fruit tart 100
Poppy-seed cake 104
Steamed chocolate pudding. 110
Sugar-crumb cake 106
Wine jelly with fruit 114

Recipe Index:German

Soups

Blumenkohlsuppe 6
Feine Kartoffelsuppe mit Gurken 5
Gaisburger Marsch.. 4
Graupensuppe mit Hühnerklein...................................... 2
Heisse Biersuppe... 4
Linsensuppe 3

Fish

Heilbutt unterm Sahneberg 10
Katerfisch 11
Rollmöpse.. 9
Zander im Ofen gebacken mit Weisswein 8
Zander Schnitte mit Senfbutter.................................... 7

Meat and Poultry

Beefsteak Tartar... 17
Berliner Hühnerfrikassee 40
Bratwurst mit saurer Sahnensosse.................................. 34
Ente mit Äpfeln und Brot Füllung.................................. 43
Falscher Wildschweinbraten 32
Gänsebraten mit Äpfeln, Rosinen und Nüssen 38
Gebratene Kalbsleber auf Berliner Art 38
Hammel Koteletten mit Zwiebelsosse................................ 25
Kalbshaxe mit Gewürzgurkensosse................................... 19
Kalbsnierenbraten 24
Kalbsrolle 22
Kasseler Rippenspeer... 31
Königsberger Klopse 14
Labskaus 37
Pichelsteiner Fleisch.. 36
Piquante Hammelschulter 26
Ragoût fin 20
Rindfleisch mit Schnittlauchsosse 15
Rouladen... 13
Sauerbraten.. 16
Schinken in Burgunder 33
Schweinerippchen mit Gewürzgurkensosse 35
Schweinskoteletten mit Knackwurst und Kartoffeln.................. 30
Sülzkoteletten 28
Süss-saure Bratwurst 34
Westfälischer Pfefferpotthast..................................... 12
Würzfleisch.. 18

Game

Fasan in Rotwein... 52
Gefüllter Fasan 53
Hasenpfeffer... 44
Piquante Rehfiletschnitten... 49
Rebhühner mit Weintrauben.. 50
Rehrücken mit Rotweinsosse... 47
Rehschnitzel mit Pilzen.. 45
Wildgeflügel mit Burgunder 51

Dumplings

Dampfnudeln.. 58
Griessklösse 59
Hefeklösse 60
Kartoffelklösse 56
Kartoffelklösse mit Pflaumenmus 57

Spätzle 55

Vegetables

Chicorée mit Schinken und Käse 68
Erbspüree 71
Gedünstetes Sauerkraut 61
Grüne Sosse 73
Grünkohl mit Kartoffeln 66
Himmel und Erde 64
Hoppelpoppel 67
Kartoffelpuffer mit Apfelmus 65
Pilze mit Tomaten und Speck 68
Rosenkohl mit Schinken und Tomaten 70
Rotkohl mit Äpfeln 63
Sauerkraut mit Ananas. 62
Saure Kartoffeln 64
Schmorgurken mit saurem Rahm und Dill 69
Weinkraut. 62
Westfälisches Blindhuhn 72

Salads

Bohnensalat 74
Lauchsalat 78
Leichter Kartoffelsalat 76
Rote Rübensalat 75
Selleriesalat mit Äpfeln 77
Warmer Kartoffelsalat mit Speck 76

Breads and Cookies

Dresdner Stollen 79
Haselnussmakronen. 82
Heidesand. 94
Honigkuchen. 88
Lebkuchen 89
Lebkuchen Häuschen 90
Mandel-Halbmonde. 86
Pfeffernüsse 85
S-Gebäck 83
Schokoladen Brezeln. 84
Springerle. 87
Spritzgebäck. 82
Weissbrot mit Kümmel. 81

Cakes and Desserts

Apfelbettelmann 109
Apfelkuchen. 108
Apfelpfannkuchen 112
Backobstkompott. 115
Frankfurter Kranz 96
Griesstorte 103
Haselnusscreme. 111
Königskuchen. 95
Mandeltorte 102
Mohnstriezel 104
Obsttorte. 100
Rauhreif. 114
Schokoladenpudding. 110
Schwarzwälder Kirschtorte. 98
Streuselkuchen. 106
Weingelee 114
Zitronencreme 113

Notes

Drawings and illustrations by Matt Greene.

Printed in U.S.A. ✖✖✖✖